The mornings at Layette's Atelier, now Kaoru's Box Meal Shop,
are like a battlefield!

"Uooohhh!!!"
Suddenly, the crowd erupted in cheers.

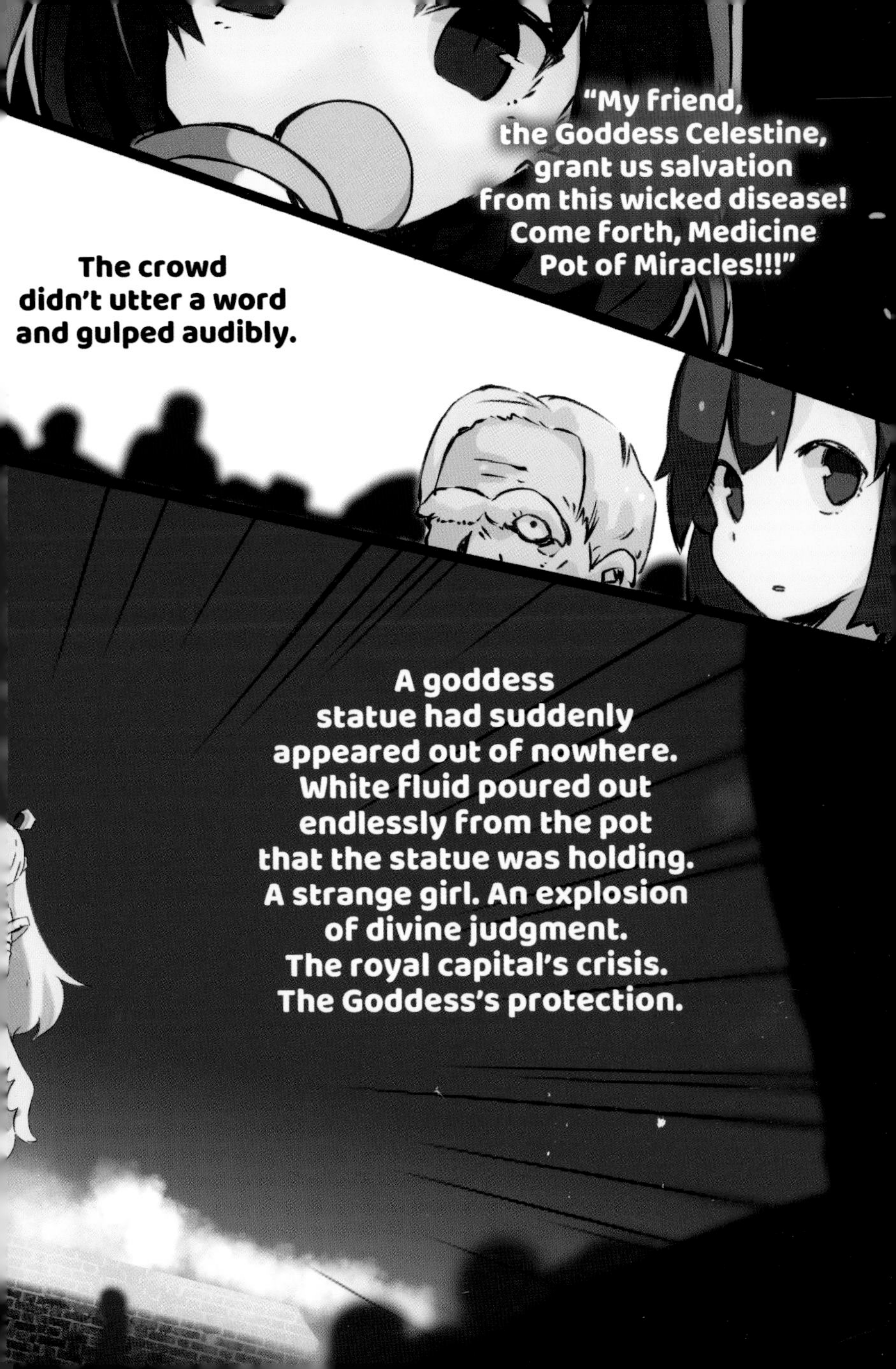
"My friend,
the Goddess Celestine,
grant us salvation
from this wicked disease!
Come forth, Medicine
Pot of Miracles!!!"
The crowd
didn't utter a word
and gulped audibly.
A goddess
statue had suddenly
appeared out of nowhere.
White fluid poured out
endlessly from the pot
that the statue was holding.
A strange girl. An explosion
of divine judgment.
The royal capital's crisis.
The Goddess's protection.

CONTENTS

I SHALL SURVIVE USING POTIONS! 3

Author FUNA Illust. Sukima

Holy Land of Rueda
Royal Capital Grua
Mountain Range
Kingdom of Balmore
Empire of Aligot
Royal Capital Aras
Drisard
Kingdom of Aseed
Kingdom of Brancott
Royal Capital Litenia
Kingdom of Jursal
N
W
E
S
design:
Mucadeya Yuko+Ogue Atsushi
(musicagographics)

I SHALL SURVIVE USING POTIONS!

3

Author: FUNA
Illustrator: Sukima

I Shall Survive Using Potions! Volume 3
by FUNA

Translated by Hiroya Watanabe
Edited by CHaSE and William Haggard
Layout by Leah Waig
English Cover & Lettering by Kelsey Denton

Illustrations by Sukima

First published in Japan in 2018 by Kodansha Ltd., Tokyo.
Publication rights for this English edition arranged through Kodansha Ltd., Tokyo.

President and Publisher: Samuel Pinansky
Managing Editor (Novels): Aimee Zink
QA Manager: Hannah N. Carter
Marketing Manager: Stephanie Hii

ISBN: 978-1-7183-7192-7
Printed in Korea
First Printing: December 2020
10 9 8 7 6 5 4 3 2 1

Chapter 21:
Layette's Atelier

A few days later...

We traveled south from Drisard, then toward the neighboring kingdom of Jusral. We had already gone east from the kingdom of Balmore to Brancott, then now Drisard, and there haven't been any signs of pursuit... Well, disregarding the lower-class nobles, who didn't know anything important. If the higher-ups got word, they'd surely try to capture us with a "polite reception" and "insist we stay," instead of calling it an arrest, but I strongly preferred to avoid all that.

To leave Drisard as soon as possible, we'd changed directions from going east, which was inland, and instead went south, where the borders were closer. The kingdom of Jusral, where we were currently located, directly neighbored Drisard, and adjacent to Brancott as well. But I doubted either of them would chase us into another kingdom, so we were relatively safe.

"We're changing plans this time. Let's get on with what I explained the other day!"

I hadn't thought it through enough last time because it had all been so sudden. I wasn't going to meet anyone new just absentmindedly wasting time at the inn, and if I were to work somewhere, doing menial tasks while staying at an expensive inn would be seen as clearly unnatural. The normal course of action would be to rent out a cheap room or find live-in work. Especially for someone like me, who's often mistaken for a minor… And at my age… I mean, my actual age! Anyway, at my age, doing simple jobs all day with actual children was too strenuous. I mean, mentally, that is.

Just then, I thought back to the beginning… When I came to this world, what did I think to accomplish? That's right, I wanted to live a carefree life with this OP power given to me by God. That's why I came up with the idea of starting a potion shop. That was a dream I'd given up on when I found out there were no magical potions in this world…

But as someone who had a four-and-a-half-year history in this world, as well as a twenty-seven-year history of being single, my knowledge of this world was already extensive. I've come to completely understand the difference between medicine with impossible effects and medicine with ordinary effects that wouldn't be out of place in this world. As long as I sold potions within that scope, there'd be no problems whatsoever.

I'd rent out a small shop, where beautiful young girls sold potions with potent, yet plausible effects, all for an affordable price. Yes, I'd create Kaoru's Atelier, a Kaoru Pharmacy! My goods would work exactly as advertised, and the cost of supplies would be zero.

The entire time, zero.

Zero, forever.

There was no way I could lose to competitors.

It'd be suspicious if there were no signs of us purchasing materials, so I'd just say Emile and Belle were tasked with gathering those ingredients for me. In addition to those duties, I'd have them hunt, gather food, and complete quests for the Hunters' Guild. They'd have a great role in generating income for living expenses, gathering information, and improving relationships, all on top of their training.

As for how we knew each other, I'd say they were two hunters I'd happened to become acquainted with, and that I provided lodging for them.

Roland and Francette? Who knows.

Actually, that might be a bit harsh… I could say that we didn't know each other, but that I'd hired them as guards, just in case. Those two could just stay at the inn. That'd be the least suspicious method.

News of the incident at the provincial city in Drisard still hadn't spread at all. It had all happened in a few seconds, and there couldn't have been more than ten or so people who saw what had actually happened up close. Besides, there was no way anyone who was there could have gotten to this region faster than we had.

Not only that, but from the kingdom of Balmore to the distant region of Drisard, which was an entire kingdom away, and to here, Jusral, the incident from four years ago was overshadowed by the news of the appearance of the Goddess, so I doubted anyone would have been talking about her messenger. Even the upper ranks shouldn't have any accurate information…

That was why any rumors of this whole incident would likely be dismissed as either an embellished story or a mistake, and would soon be forgotten. Even if it did reach the upper ranks, they'd just search within the kingdom, or assume we'd headed east and search in that direction.

In other words, no one would come looking this way. I highly doubted they'd spread this story to the other kingdoms.

Conclusion: I was safe here. And tomorrow, I'd finally arrive at the royal capital, Litenia.

The royal capital, a populous melting pot of people from across the land, was the best place to set up shop inconspicuously. A forest was the best place to hide a leaf, and the most chaotic city of the kingdom was the best place to hide a person.

"Okay, everyone, tomorrow we proceed as planned!"

"...Is it really going to work?"

"I'm worried..."

Roland and Francette were being downers already, but I had it all figured out this time!

"This again? I told you, it'll be fine! We'll be sleeping in proper beds starting tomorrow, so let's enjoy our last night camping and go to sleep already."

Roland and Francette looked at me with reproachful eyes. I called it camping, but I brought out the baron's bed from before and climbed in with Layette. Yeah, this bed has been really useful in the past four and a half years...

*　　*

"It's the royal capital..."

The next day, we arrived at Litenia and passed through the city gates, sticking to the backstories we'd been using. The other two pairs, Roland and Francette, and Emile and Belle, may have gotten through without issue with this updated story, but I was afraid Layette and I would be taken aside for questioning. That was why I decided to save the new backstories for once we were inside the royal capital.

Yup, there was no need to shoulder problems unnecessarily.

Once we got enough distance from the gate, we split up into three groups. We were to act like complete strangers until we "happened to meet up" later on. We'd all find separate lodgings, as well.

"...So how did we end up at the same inn?!"

"Well, I just randomly picked a place, and you happened to be here..."

"...Likewise."

So said Roland and Emile. Judging by the looks on their faces, they didn't seem to be lying...

But considering we had split up from the same spot, went elsewhere at staggered times, then walked down the main road toward the center of the city, it wasn't too farfetched to end up at the same inn. They'd been staying at inns of my choosing so far, so they'd gotten accustomed to a certain quality of lodging, too...

I mean, over half of us were young girls, so I wanted to avoid any shady locations. I also didn't want to stay anywhere with bad food, and it had to be a certain level of quality since we were supposed to be nobles. But I had to avoid places that high-class nobles and big merchants might stay at, and it had to have a nice ambiance, so the first inn that caught my eye... Well, that explained why we all ended up here.

"Not much we can do about that now... But we're still strangers until we all officially meet up. So, at least while we're here, let's not interact any more than normal guests would."

After our hushed discussion away from the inn workers and other guests, I went back to my room with Layette.

* *

Four days later...

Layette and I were sitting at the shop counter. No, not just any shop—our shop.

The medicine shop, Layette's Atelier.

Kaoru's Atelier would've been a bit much, it'd make it easier for "those people" to find me, and I didn't want anyone to think I was using the messenger's name. Most of all, I chose the name because I wanted Layette to know she had a home she could always come back to.

...Though I did have other reasons, too.

"Pharmacy" might have been a more apt name, but I've always liked the sound of "atelier" because it sounds like an alchemical workshop. I was also worried that we'd get regular customers if I named it a pharmacy.

What's that? How did I get the shop set up so quickly, you ask? It wasn't like this was modern Japan. There wasn't any tedious paperwork to fill out. No residence card, seal certificate, or guarantor was needed, either. Just the deposit and an advance payment for rent. That was it. I guess, as long as I pay, it doesn't matter if I go bankrupt and flee in the night or hang myself.

...Not that I'd do any of those things!

In any case, the first realtor mocked me, thinking I was a child, so I left immediately. The second one treated me as a proper customer as soon as I showed them some gold, and I signed the contract for this shop-slash-residence. It used to be a general store, apparently. It was a two-story building where the first floor contained a shop, a small warehouse (or more like a storeroom), a kitchen, washroom, and toilet.

The washroom didn't have a shower or bathtub or anything like that, just a portable laundry tub for bringing hot water in from the kitchen, which could be used to wipe yourself down.

The toilet wasn't the type that flushed either. It was just a po... *No, I don't wanna say it!*

My Item Box eliminated the need for a warehouse, but it'd be better to keep some stock in there for appearance's sake. I'd work out what to do with the rest of the space later.

Unlike a general store, I only needed a few shelves for the shop section, so I took out a ton of the shelves that were already in there to make room for a table and four chairs. I then decorated the display shelves with glass containers and ornaments. They were, of course, created with my ability and up for sale, so I purposely lowered the quality upon making these.

The window was originally just a wooden one, but I had a craftsman upgrade it to double-paned glass, keeping the original wooden parts intact and adding an interior glass window. The wooden window could only be opened or closed before, but now I had the option of using the glass. Well, I'd made the glass with my ability. It'd probably fetch a nice price for the quality.

The curtains were purchased normally at a store. I mean, I shouldn't be using my abilities for everything. I did have a duty to contribute to the economy, being a member of society and all. The only times I'd use my abilities were when there were no other options, and when I didn't feel like using another method.

...As such, I used my powers to make the lighting fixtures. Yeah, I'm too easy on myself! So what? The lighting was the face and signboard of the shop. I absolutely couldn't skimp on that! If I'd used candles or an oil lamp, I'd have to worry about odors and the risk of fire.

I'd only keep the shop open during the day, but I made the lighting look like normal lamps (I made them self-contained fixtures with a power supply that would last about thirty years.) I may have just been renting it, but it was my first shop... my castle. Of course I was going to be picky! Haah... haah...

So, the sections that required water and any areas that needed goods to be carried in and out often were on the first floor, and the second floor was for living space. It was just me and Layette for now, but I had rooms ready for Emile and Belle to move in, too.

"Okay, let's do this! I'm going to use this shop to make some money, get to know more people, and find myself a marriage partner! For my happiness, and for the growth of the Nagase clan in this world!"

Upon hearing this, Layette muttered to herself, "I'm not sure what she's talking about, but I'm kinda worried… I should be more responsible…"

What's that supposed to mean?!

* *

"Layette's Atelier? Some sort of workshop?"

A shop had suddenly appeared where the closed-down general store had previously been. There hadn't been any signs of construction beforehand, so it clearly must've been purchased with everything included. In these cases, the interior and equipment from the previous tenant were transferred to the new owner, making it possible to open a new business much faster than if everything was to be replaced, but, in turn, the equipment would all be used. Though this was more of an issue on the business side, so it didn't really affect the customers.

Many were surprised by the appearance of a store that had opened in just a matter of days, but they were further taken aback upon peering into the building.

"…There are only children working here."

In this world, 157cm was the average height of a twelve-year-old girl. And despite the rather unpleasant look in Kaoru's eyes, her face looked rather child-like, overall. In addition, those of Asian ethnicity seemed particularly young from the Western-ish population's point of view. So, no matter who looked at her, Kaoru absolutely looked like a little kid.

There was a sign put up outside the shop, with some text written just below the shop's name.

"We have all types of medicine in stock. We will also compound specific types upon request."

"No way…"

They were clearly just children. It wasn't as if they were selling cookies or anything. How could children be trusted to handle sales of expensive, difficult-to-handle medicine, which could cause serious issues if there were any errors…? Ineffective folk medicines were one thing, but even some folk medicines were quite powerful in their efficacy and side effects alike.

If they were indeed selling something that could easily be obtained by the average commoner, it'd be unlikely that the store would make enough profit to stay afloat. They were called "folk medicines" because they were easily obtainable and safe to use by the common folk, after all. Although they were often thought to be similar, folk medicine is very different from the likes of herbal and galenical medicine.

About ten people were now gathered at the corner of the side street. Finally, one of them resolved to set foot inside. The others followed, entering the shop one by one.

Cling…

The doorbell rang, and the young girls working there responded at once.

"Welcome!"

"Welcone!"

...Layette had messed it up. And the guests who'd entered all nearly died from the moe shock.

They struggled to contain themselves at how cute the girls were, and began browsing the wares in the store.

Since it was originally a general store, it was quite roomy compared to most stores of this type. It was unlikely any sort of medicine being sold at an individually owned store would be much good. Even including shady, crude drugs that might not even technically qualify as actual medicine, there weren't very many kinds of medicine out there. Rare and expensive drugs were usually stored in a safe at the back of the shop or handled via special order only, and many of them could only be purchased by nobles or royalty.

"Healing medicine for soldier's disease...?"

After some time, one of the men read the description on a shelf out loud: "Soldier's disease." Upon hearing this, most modern-day people would likely think of Legionnaires' disease, a deadly illness caused by bacteria known as Legionella pneumophila. Besides that, it's a bit dated, but there was also beriberi...

In any case, "soldier's disease" in this place referred to...

"This can make that unbearable itchiness better?"

Yes, it's athlete's foot. It wasn't limited to soldiers, but it was incredibly common among the ranks, as many who were originally healthy had become afflicted as soon as they joined the military. It wasn't hard to imagine why it became known as the soldier's disease.

"Oh, yes, that's right. Just as it says there, there are three types of medicine, and the one worth three small silver coins can prevent itchiness by applying it once a day. It'll prevent it from getting any worse. The kind worth three silver will prevent itchiness and slowly cure the condition. And finally, the one worth three small gold coins will cure it within a few days. But do keep in mind that we are not responsible if it recurs again after being cured."

Three small silver coins was equivalent to about 300 yen. This may sound cheap, but anyone who began using it would never be able to stop, and the itchiness never got cured, so it was quite wicked in design. Although it relieved itchiness and prevented it from getting worse, it was devilish in the way it continually drained money from its user.

Even if it was cured with the expensive medicine, they could always get it again from someone else; if they didn't change out the shoes or mat they were using previously, they'd *definitely* get it again. It was a medicine that continued to sell and bring in profits forever. A well of never-ending gold.

...She was pure evil.

"Is it really going to work...?"

The man seemed skeptical, and no one could blame him. There was no way such effective medicine would be sold at a store run by little girls. It was probably no better than applying some plants you'd find outside...

But the man reconsidered. They may be little girls, but considering they had the funds to rent out a store like this, they had to have some sort of sponsor backing them. There were probably people in charge of purchasing and other aspects of the business, and these girls were simply working the counter. And since they had gone to the trouble of opening the shop, they had to be expecting the wares to produce a profit. In other words, they must've been worth selling.

There was no harm in trying. It was merely three small silver coins, which was about the price of breakfast. Even if it didn't work, it was no big loss.

"These are for diarrhea and constipation, huh..." Another man was looking at two medicine bottles.

Many of the residents of this kingdom, particularly those in the royal capital, had a diet mainly consisting of meat. Since they didn't consume enough fiber, many were afflicted with constipation. Though, not eating enough meat could also lead to constipation… Kaoru had been researching this very topic the past few days.

"There's medicine for healing wounds, treating stomach pain and curing hangovers… I haven't heard of many treatments for hangovers before."

I'd been observing each of the customers. Indeed, this shop didn't sell medicine to treat anything too serious. Human lives could be on the line if medicine for serious illnesses didn't work, and even if they did work, that'd bring unwanted attention as well.

Nobles, royalty, merchants, thugs… All sorts of crowds would gather at the store. That'd be a pain to deal with, and it'd interfere with my search for a husband.

I wasn't looking to marry someone who was attracted to the potions I made. My potions were for securing my safety and happiness, and giving a little help to people who suffered from injuries and illnesses. It absolutely wasn't something to be given out in unlimited quantities or for helping the rich and powerful.

That was why this shop wouldn't handle medicine with grand effects that would catch the attention of those in power, be a matter of life or death, have any political value, or be potentially profitable enough that the rich would want to take them from me. I'd only handle low-key medicines that the commoners would appreciate.

The prices were cheap; that is, besides the select few that were for milking those big earners. I mean, the cost of the goods was zero, after all.

I also had various types of glass bottles, pottery, ornamental containers, perfumes, skin lotions, cosmetic serums, and milky lotions. There'd be quite a bit of open shelf space with just medicine, and it'd be better to have something to sell when there were no injured or sick to cure. Besides, women were willing to pay big money for the sake of beauty.

"I'll take one of these."

A man seemed willing to give the low-grade treatment for soldier's disease a try, and purchased it for three small silver coins.

"Thank you!"

"T-Tank you!"

...Layette messed it up again. Was she doing it on purpose to be cute?

After that, a line formed in front of the counter. It was unclear whether everyone was celebrating the opening of a shop run by young children, or if they were curious to see if the medicine was effective. In any case, Layette's Atelier was off to a good start, with sales already on their first day in business.

Chapter 22: Novice Hunter

"I'd like to turn this in, please."

"Right, thanks."

Emile placed an item at the exchange counter of the Hunters' Guild, which the guild worker accepted.

Emile and Belle had been working as novice hunters for the last few days. Emile hadn't missed a day of sword training since that day four years ago. When Kaoru had approached Emile and Belle when they were street urchins and asked, "How would you two like to help me, as my servants?" he'd decided to become her sword and shield... And, although his style was his own, he'd actually become somewhat proficient.

He'd used a wooden sword for training at first, but Kaoru got him a practice sword and then a real sword upon finding this out. He'd been training from early morning to late at night, outside of the time he spent to make money and take care of the young ones. He had a goal that was more important than his own life. With such intense training, there was no way he wouldn't improve.

Natural talent? An efficient training regiment? A capable training instructor? None of that mattered to a demon.

When Kaoru had realized Emile's self-taught swordsmanship had no regard for protecting himself and solely focused on defeating the enemy and shielding others with his own body, she'd gotten flustered and forced him to find a swordmaster to train under. It was run by a retired veteran hunter who'd trained others as a hobby, but

Emile was trained in the way of the sword and in mental fortitude as well, and was now able to call himself a fully-fledged swordsman.

More important than his improvement with the sword was that he'd learned that there'd be no one to protect those he cared about if he sacrificed himself for their sake. True service meant ensuring his own survival in order to continue protecting others.

And so, Emile had learned to think about his own survival, as well.

Emile was now quite skilled in combat against human opponents for his age, but that was strictly against other humans. He wasn't able to hunt the swift horned rabbits, take down flying birds, or kill a boar. Essentially, he could only escort others or gather materials, making him quite inflexible as a hunter. This meant the jobs he could take on were quite limited.

As for Belle, the extent of her fighting abilities was limited to tackling and stabbing someone with the knife she was hiding. She could hardly be counted on for combat.

Despite their shortcomings, there were those who would invite them to their party. Though, of course, they were far from the respectable kind. Their goal was to have Emile die quickly so they could share Belle amongst themselves. Even if they didn't kill him directly, it'd be easy for the rest of the party to coordinate and put him in a dangerous situation. Whether Emile was aware of this or not, he'd avoided accepting such offers.

Within the past few days, they'd become known as a new, but not stupid, straitlaced-as-hell brother and sister duo. The two had been living together for as long as they could remember, so anyone who saw them thought they were as close as brother and sister.

Right when Emile received his payment for the herbs and food ingredients he had collected, "it" appeared…

Clang...

The door opened along with the ring of the door bell, and the hunters reflexively turned toward that direction. This was none other than a hunter's instinct.

Then...

Twitch!

Everyone flinched at once. A little embarrassed, they soon relaxed and went back to what they were doing, whether it was talking or eating...

The person who'd walked into the guild was just a little girl. The hunters who'd flinched at her arrival all felt shamed by their own reactions. Even though it was only for a moment, they'd gotten scared by the look in the girl's eyes...

As for the girl, she had an unconcerned expression on her face. It wasn't that she didn't feel it was unpleasant... she'd just gotten used to it. That was all.

She continued walking toward the quest counter with purpose.

"Please process this."

With that, she handed a piece of paper to the receptionist girl that read:

"Guards wanted.

Duration: Until the client or contractor wishes to end the terms.

Reward: One small gold coin per day.

Number of People: 2

Conditions: Both must be in a party, and one or both of them must be female."

"Huh...?" The receptionist couldn't help but react upon receiving the form. "E-Excuse me, about the listed conditions..." She seemed to be flustered about having to mention something that went without saying. So she explained hesitantly to the little girl, "Um, I don't think there will be any party that will accept this request with these conditions... You won't be charged the commission if no one accepts it, but it will still incur the quest registration fee. Would it be possible to soften the conditions...?"

"No, this is all the reward I can give. And we're all women, so I won't accept a party unless it's only women as well, or a man and a woman. If no one takes the offer, I will decide what to do then."

She couldn't refuse to take it at that point; she had tried to advise the little girl. Therefore, she'd completed her duty and acted entirely in good faith.

With that in mind, the receptionist proceeded to do her job. And so, a new request card was put up on the board.

"What the...?!"

"A small gold coin for two people? That'd barely pay for a room and meal. Who'd wanna take this?"

The hunters all laughed upon seeing the request.

"To top it off, it's an escort job. That's gonna take up way too much time. They should've at least checked the market price before posting this..."

After the laughter went on for some time, a two-person party walked up to the request board, read the card, then peeled it off.

"What...?"

They walked away from the surprised group of hunters and approached the receptionist.

"We'll take this."

"Huh...?" The receptionist looked at them in disbelief with her mouth ajar. "...Oh, e-excuse me! Um, you can accept it, of course, but the client is still here, so you may want to check the details with her now."

The boy and girl nodded, and the receptionist called over a young girl.

"I'm Kaoru, the client and owner of Layette's Atelier. The conditions are just as they're written there: One small gold coin per person, per day, and this will be a live-in job. Food expenses, consumables, and other miscellaneous expenses will all be provided. The knowledge that hunters live with us as bodyguards will be enough of a deterrent, so unless I specifically request something, you are free to take on any other jobs. Do you have any questions?"

"None. We're Emile and Belle. We may be novice hunters, but it'd be an honor to serve you."

"Yes, thank you for your service."

"Whaaat?!" the others shouted from all around them.

"They get a small gold coin each?!"

"Food expenses are paid for and they're free to take other jobs? They basically got a place to stay for free!"

"No way... But I guess if she needed a two-person party with a woman, we didn't qualify, anyway."

There might have been resentment if there had been other qualifying parties, but with having a woman as part of the party as one of the prerequisites, they settled down with a few envious comments.

I had a reason for taking such a roundabout method, of course. It would've been suspicious for someone to take the request card without reading its contents, as well as if someone else had happened to meet the conditions and took the card first. But it would've also been strange if the conditions were too unfavorable, not to mention how bad that would've been for Emile and Belle's future prospects. That's why I made it a great deal that seemed bad at first glance, making them seem like quick-witted and observant hunters.

In any case, Emile and Belle were now officially residents of Layette's Atelier. They simply had to help out at the store and continue improving as hunters from then on. Then, once we parted ways, they'd be able to return to the kingdom of Balmore and live on protecting the orphans of the Eyes of the Goddess.

I couldn't have them traveling with me forever. Emile and Belle both had their own lives, and I wanted them to take care of themselves.

...They didn't plan on staying with me even after I got married, did they?

* *

I gave one of the rooms on the second floor to Emile and Belle, and we began our life together with the four of us. They'd be sharing a room, but they'd been living like brother and sister since childhood, so it was no big deal. After all, they had lived together in that dilapidated, one-room building that could barely withstand the elements. And now, they were partners.

...Though I didn't think that pushover Emile had it in him to make a move on Belle, who was still twelve years old and like a younger sister to him. Besides, if I'd split them up, Emile may not have said anything, but Belle might have been upset.

In any case, things were going as planned, so far. Francette and the others were next, but we were sure to "meet" them soon. For now, they could spend some time in their room flirting with each other.

Urgh, some day, I'll also…

As our post-late-breakfast break ended, it was time to open up the shop.

"Time to get ready."

"Okay!" Layette answered from atop my lap.

Belle stared at us with an envious look in her eyes. I hoped she knew she was much heavier than me. I'd get crushed… It would've been a different story four years ago, when we'd just met, but…

Emile's group went off to the guild to find more work. I went down to the first floor with Layette, opened the curtains, then opened the inner glass window. Once I opened that window and the outer wooden one…

"Whoa!"

…Ah, oops.

I was supposed to say, "Kya!" I'm so bad at being girly…

No, now isn't the time for that! The heck is this?!

There were nearly twenty people gathered outside.

Wait… are they all customers?

I mean, there were about ten people who had visited out of curiosity before, and it had been pretty slow since, so why?

I composed myself and locked the wooden window open, closed the glass window, opened the door, and…

"Welcome!"

"W-Welcan!"

Layette, you're doing that on purpose, aren't you? You usually speak pretty clearly… Ohh, you sly child!

"I'll take some medicine for soldier's disease!"

"Me too!"

"I-I'll take some too!"

Ahh, look at all these people who needed my drugs to go on!

…Just as planned!

"I'll take the one worth three silver."

"Me too."

"Me three!"

It seemed they'd realized the medicine was effective, so they wanted to cure the condition instead of getting temporary relief. Though, even if they were cured, they'd probably get it again because everyone else around them had it, and they probably weren't going to change their shoes anytime soon.

I figured there were more buyers now because people were beginning to see the effects for other people, or they had tried some of their friends'. In any case, I was glad to see it gaining publicity.

"I'll take three."

"Same here."

"I'll take five."

Huh?

"Um, you'll get better with just one. You could purchase another one if it happens to come back, so isn't five four too many?"

"Oh, I'm going to earn some points with my boss by giving him a bottle as a gift."

"I'm getting a bottle for Eliza."

"Hey, you bastard!"

"I'm going to resell them at wor— Er, never mind."

Like hell you are!

"...Only two per person! This is a pharmacy and a retail shop. We do not do wholesale!"

They began arguing and blaming each other, but they settled down and left with two bottles each when I threatened to reduce the limit to one.

"I'll take one diarrhea and one constipation medicine."

"Huh? Why do you need medicine for opposite symptoms?"

Normally, sales associates shouldn't infringe on a customer's privacy. But... this was a pharmacy, after all. Since I was selling medicine, there were some things I just couldn't let pass. I wouldn't allow someone to use them in a way I didn't agree with.

"Well, my diet tends to get unbalanced when I travel to different regions and get food, and sometimes there's weird stuff in there. I get constipated at first, then the next day, it's like an explos—"

"Thankyouforyourpurchase!"

"Tank you!"

Our sales continued increasing. I was selling medicine for stomach pain, toothache, and general pain relief, as well. But if those were signs of more serious illnesses, there was a chance that masking the pain would lead to the issue getting worse without the patient's knowledge. To prevent that, I added an effect that would halt the progression of the illness while the pain reliever was in effect. I didn't make it fully cure an illness, since that would garner the attention of more powerful and sinister people. It was just to maintain the patient's current status.

Curing malignant diseases wasn't a job for medicine from Layette's Atelier, but for the blessing of the Goddess herself: the Tears of the Goddess. Eventually, I planned on having Emile and Belle resume work as the Eyes of the Goddess and find those who were worthy of having the blessings of the Goddess bestowed upon them.

Though all this wouldn't be done all at once, of course. It wasn't as if everyone who was deserving of the Goddess's blessing would receive it. Only a select few, who happened to be very lucky, would get it.

Gods are fickle creatures. The Goddess of this world, in particular…

Chapter 23: The Officer

"Is this the place?"

"Yes, sir!"

I was enjoying my time with Layette, since there were no customers around, when I heard a brisk voice from outside the shop. Most kids would get scared and run away when they saw my face, so it'd been over ten years since I could play with one! What was the harm in spending a little time… Oh, I guess there were more important things at hand, huh.

I had a bad feeling about this… And my "bad feelings" had the unfortunate tendency to be right.

What's that? It's not just a "feeling" at this point? Huh, maybe that was why they tended to be right.

"Layette, go hide upstairs."

"Okay!"

Without hesitation, Layette went running upstairs, just as she was told. It wasn't that I was being cold to her, but rather that I'd taught her time and time again that it was important to follow my orders in these situations, because the slightest delay could put me at a disadvantage. In other words, obeying my orders as soon as possible was Layette's way of showing her loyalty to me.

Clang…

"Is this the shop known as Layette's Atelier?"

"Yes it is. Can I help you?"

The man who rang the doorbell as he entered was obviously military personnel; not just a common foot soldier, but someone higher in rank. There were some more military men behind him… younger in appearance, and clearly a lower rank than him.

"Is the owner here?"

"Yes, that would be me."

"What…? Oh, no, that's not what I meant. I'm not asking for the current person in charge, but the main proprietor of the business."

"As I said, that would be me. Signing the lease, paying the rent, purchasing the goods, selling them, and being harassed by military men is all my responsibility."

"Wha…"

I wasn't sure if his second surprised reaction was from the fact that I was the owner, or because he was being talked back to by a child.

"So you're Layette?"

"No…?"

"Huh?" They all had blank expressions on their faces.

I didn't name it "Layette's Atelier" instead of "Kaoru's Atelier" just for this sort of reaction! I think…

"Just don't think about it too much… It's just a name!"

I had a feeling he'd demand to see Layette if I told him there was someone else by that name, so I quickly made up an excuse.

"Oh, I see… Then let me ask you something. Can you tell me in detail about the medicine being sold here that cures soldier's disease?"

Huh? That was what he wanted to ask about? Why was a military officer asking about some plain old medicine for athlete's foot?

"Well, there's not much to say, it's just medicine… The supplier and manufacturing methods are trade secrets. If you're going to tell me to give those up, I'll have to ask you about classified military information in return."

"What! Well… I suppose you have a point."

I thought he'd get angry with me, but he responded to my coldness with a bitter smile. Maybe he was a surprisingly reasonable person?

"Then let me change the question. Is it possible to purchase this medicine in bulk?"

If he was here for business, that was another story.

Customer service smile, customer service smile… Why are they all pulling back? Pisses me off!

…Well, I'm used to it by now, having lived with this face for twenty-seven years.

"Certainly, though my supplier does have a limit. Oh, and the army will not be able to replicate it. Even if they learn the manufacturing method, we certainly aren't making excessive profits with these prices. If you gather the ingredients, separate them, boil them, refine them, mix them, then boil them again all at the army, it will likely be much more costly than purchasing the stock here. Though I doubt you'd know how to find the herbs required to make it in the first place. You'd need to know not just the region, but which trees to check, or whether they're at the riverside, in the forest, at mountain top, or in the sandy soil…"

"I suspected as much. It was highly doubtful you were making much profit at all, selling them at three small silver coins a bottle. In fact, you're in the red with just the price of the bottles alone… Though I'm sure the cheap ones are for gaining publicity, and serve as bait to get them to buy the more expensive medicine…"

Wow, impressive! He read into the excuse I'd prepared in case someone asked about this! Well, I supposed anyone could figure that out, unless they were an idiot.

I'd considered raising the prices and offering partial refunds for trading in the bottles, but decided against it. I didn't want to take back any bottles they'd touched with the same hands they'd rubbed all over their athlete's foot! Who in their right mind would?! I was helping them with the cheapest option by providing a measure of relief for those who didn't have much money anyway.

Hm? How was I helping them when I'd be draining money from them for the rest of their lives? Because I'd be giving them motivation to work in order to buy more medicine. Be a NEET no more! I was really, definitely helping them by giving them that extra push. It was a certified act of charity.

It'd also help my financial situation at the same time, so the relief went both ways.

"Though, even three silver coins isn't expensive by any means. The bottle priced at three silver coins would recoup the losses from the lowest tier, then the customer works their way up to the bottle priced at one small gold coin, where you must be gaining your profits..."

Such an astute analysis! He wasn't an officer for nothing!

...Too bad he was completely wrong. Though, I figured no one else could create unlimited bottles and medicine for free, so I couldn't blame him.

"Ahaha, well... Oh, that reminds me. If too much of the medicine is being made, the plants necessary to make the medicine may be wiped out in this region. That may force me to relocate in search of a new place to harvest the ingredients..."

The officer visibly frowned. Just how much of it was he planning to buy…?

In any case, that should've prevented him from placing orders in unreasonable quantities or asking about the manufacturing method. Good thing I'd come up with excuses beforehand just in case…

"Then how many bottles can you provide per day?"

"What? Per day?"

That'd be rather inconvenient. Making the medicine wasn't an issue, but I'd already told the other customers purchases were limited to two per person, and it'd be annoying to deal with a mob of soldiers coming to my shop every day.

What to do…

Oh, I had something to ask first.

"Um, are you the military officers for the royal army?"

I had to confirm who these soldiers were. Hopefully they were part of the medical team of the royal army. If not…

"Ah, I apologize. I'd been asking so many questions without even introducing myself. I'm the second battalion commander of the royal army, Lieutenant Colonel Vonsas. These two are my corporals, Tyde and Mericus."

"What…?"

I was aghast. Not only was he not part of the medical unit, judging by his title, but…

"U-Um, how many battalions does the royal army have? And how many officers are…"

If I'd asked these questions of military personnel on Earth, I may have been questioned under suspicion of being a spy. But in this world, the number of soldiers wasn't something you could really hide, and it was something to be flaunted with pride rather than be kept a secret. The citizens of the kingdom and neighboring countries were sure to know this information already, so I doubted it'd be a problem now.

"Ah, the royal army consists of ten battalions, totaling 10,000 men. Though a little less than half of them aren't combat personnel, but rather support troops, such as transport soldiers and administrative officers."

As expected, the lieutenant colonel seemed unconcerned as he described the size of the army. He seemed to realize I knew next to nothing about the army and went into great detail for me, too. Maybe he thought this would be necessary knowledge for doing business in the royal capital and was lecturing me out of kindness, or maybe he realized why I was asking the question…

It was probably the latter. He must have suspected what I'd be asking next.

The lieutenant colonel explained that, in the royal army, squads consisted of nine soldiers, and squads were the smallest type of unit. Forty men consisting of four squads, a platoon leader, and three assisting corporals made up a platoon. Four platoons made up one company, and 640 men consisting of four companies plus personnel from the command division and supporting personnel made up one battalion. There were ten battalions, from the first to tenth. He also added that there were other divisions, such as transportation, training, instruction, and other such supporting and subsidiary branches. With all of those people combined, there were about 10,000 men in total. There were ten times the number of citizens that they had to look after.

Though this wasn't just any capital city, but the royal capital itself. Goods, money, and personnel came here from throughout the kingdom. The king had direct control over the area and the army here, and the royal army had to protect more than just the royal capital. The troops headed by the lords of each region were unique in a variety of ways. The lieutenant colonel's explanation had confirmed my apprehensions.

"So this means the royal army has nine other battalions, with nine battalion commanders, who are of equal rank to you…? Would there be a chance that they'll all come to this shop demanding the remedy for soldier's disease?"

"Absolutely. I doubt they would come in person, but I can say with certainty they would send their subordinates."

"Whaaat!"

What nonsense is he saying with such a straight face?!

"D-Does this mean I'm going to have this conversation nine more times? With people who will insist I prioritize sending medicine to them?"

"Oh, I'm sure of it. We may be a part of the same army, but the battalions are all rivals. We all want to secure any good product available for ourselves. And this wouldn't be limited to the battalions; I assume companies and platoons will come in individually as well."

"Whaaat?!"

This is bad…

This lieutenant colonel seemed respectable enough, but I suspected there were people in the army who were pushy and believed every citizen should automatically obey them. If people like that began demanding I supply them with all my medicine, it'd be difficult to deal with. Not to mention that my shop would be overflowing with soldiers if even a small unit of them decided to visit at once. I didn't want to get involved in all this, and I definitely didn't want to deal with arguments between different units.

A civil war within the royal army. The cause? Medicine for athlete's foot. The girl who was the root of all this gets executed as a spy from another kingdom.

Arrrgh!

I began panicking at the horrifying thought as the lieutenant colonel spoke to me.

"Don't worry. This is why I, a battalion commander, took the time to come here in person. The other units will likely send over a corporal or someone of a similar rank, so you can tell them you're making deliveries under the orders from Lieutenant Colonel Vonsas, the second battalion commander, and direct them to me. I doubt anyone would be willing to challenge you after that. I don't plan on hoarding it all for myself, so you know. I will distribute it to everyone else for the base price. I would only ask the other battalions for small favors in other fields."

...How dirty! So this must have been how he climbed the ranks in the army!

But something just came across my mind...

"Um, what if someone from another unit came in as a normal customer instead of a representative of the army?"

"What?"

"What?"

"Whaaat?!"

It seemed the lieutenant colonel wasn't so impressive after all...

After discussing it further with him, I ended up deciding to refuse sale to any customers who tried to buy in bulk as a representative of their unit, and anyone who came to purchase as an individual would be limited to two bottles. He agreed to put out an official notice stating soldiers could only purchase the soldier's disease medicine through military channels. Otherwise, I wouldn't be able to deal with the long line of soldiers that would surely form in front of my shop every day. There may be those who would sneakily buy some in civilian clothes, but I didn't mind if it was just a few of them. So long as they didn't obstruct my business, they wouldn't be too big of a problem.

If they did do something like that, their colleagues, seniors, and superiors would find out and punish them, so I doubted many would attempt it. The lieutenant colonel said they could get medicine and treatments from the military medical unit for free, so there shouldn't be too many people willing to go through all that just to spend money out of their own pocket. I didn't know how reliable the predictions of a noble-born elite field officer were, but all I could do was pray he was right.

As well, I'd deliver the second battalion's orders once a week. It was a bit hard to sell in bulk at my shop after explicitly saying we were a retailer and not wholesale, since I had to consider how it'd make me look. Besides, I wanted to go out and about sometimes, instead of being cooped up in my shop all the time.

Though, secretly, I was thinking how the military HQ would probably have plenty of young, elite soldiers, and meeting a bunch of people could be beneficial for finding someone to marry. It'd also be helpful for my safety if soldiers memorized my face and decided they wanted to protect me.

Very helpful, indeed...

If something were to happen to me, the supply of their medicine would be cut off. They probably would've ignored me if some punk was bothering me on the streets, but they'd definitely help me out if they knew me.

Wait, does this mean the 10,000 men in the royal army are now my personal bodyguards? This is too amazing! Roland and the others are completely unnecessary now! Muahaha!

"I'll be counting on you, then!"

With that, the lieutenant colonel and his men departed. Right after, Roland and Francette entered.

"Was there trouble?"

It seemed Roland had been watching over me from outside the whole time. He probably intended to charge in if anything happened to me.

I'm sorry for thinking you were useless.

"It's okay, just business talk. Thanks."

I'd at least give him some words of appreciation. I didn't know how long he'd been out there, after all. Francette could've even been out there all night… Just kidding, ahaha…

Wait a minute… Francette? What's with that sleepy-looking face and yawn just now? And are those bags under your eyes?!

Whoa, whoa, whoa, whoa, whoa, whoa! L-Let's just go ahead and drink some of this, Fran. No, no, just shut up and drink it!

•

In the evening…

A carriage stopped in front of the store, after which its passengers entered

"…Hey, is there where that soldier's disease medicine is being sold?"

A married couple, who were obviously nobility and seemed to be about thirty or so, and their two attendants, all came inside.

"Yes, can I help you…?"

I missed my chance to have Layette flee upstairs. With no other option left, I tapped her head as a signal to have her keep quiet and fade into the background.

"All right, give me everything you've got. You will be sending everything you get in stock from here on out, as well. The price will be 30% off."

"I decline."

"Good. Then first, give me… H-Huh?"

The customer's eyes went wide, as if he hadn't expected a mere commoner to dare refuse his command. He was probably planning to monopolize my medicine and sell it to the army for a profit or use it for some sort of political advantage… But wait, why would some freakin' medicine for athlete's foot be so important?! Were we talking about war material here?

In any case, no way was I letting him take off 30% just like that. Sure, I didn't incur any cost for the ingredients, but that was just by coincidence. Now that I considered myself a merchant, I wasn't going to let him walk all over me like that. Haggling was a vital part of any business transaction, so I was willing to oblige him, though whether we would strike a deal was a different story.

Trying to force a deal was out of the question. Completely unacceptable.

I'd be putting an end to that real fast. I could hardly call myself a merchant if I ever accepted such a thing. I only spent about half a year working in my previous life, but I had a high sense of pride in my work and camaraderie with my colleagues.

"H-How dare you! You think you can get away with opposing…"

"Bulk purchases of the medicine for soldier's disease are being handled by Lieutenant Colonel Vonsas of the royal army's second battalion. Please direct any such inquiries to him. I'd also like to add that we have an agreement, so any actions that would obstruct the army's purchase of medicine will be reported to the lieutenant colonel, and he will be taking care of all such issues…"

"Wh-What?! You mean Lieutenant Colonel Nevas von Vonsas, third son of Count Vonsas…?"

"I'm not familiar with his full name, but yes, it is Lieutenant Colonel Vonsas, the second battalion leader."

The nobles went silent for some time, then turned around to leave. I quickly called after them.

"Excuse me, madam, would you care for some hair wash or facial remedies while you're here?"

"What?"

I wasn't keen on making enemies, so I didn't really want them to leave in a bad mood. Plus, I wanted to take the opportunity to start selling the cosmetic stuff that had been sitting on the shelf. I was pretty confident that once people began buying and using those products, they'd serve as real-world advertisements and lead to even more sales.

"This medicine removes dirt from your hair and makes it silky smooth, and this one moisturizes your skin! With these, you can regain the appearance of youthfulness!"

I gave the wife a sales pitch you might hear from a cosmetics salesperson at some department store. She was about at that age where women began worrying about their declining looks.

She paused. "I do wonder if you're telling the truth… Do you understand what would happen if you deceive a noble? You wouldn't be forgiven just because you are a child."

It sounded too good to be true… A small-time shop being tended by a child couldn't possibly have such a miracle medicine…

Even with these thoughts in mind, it seemed she couldn't resist my enticing words. The fact that her noble husband took his time to visit my shop probably helped support the notion that it sold medicine of value, as well.

I left Layette behind the counter and walked out to the floor of the shop. "Please look at my hair."

The wife looked at my head with a dubious expression, ran her fingers through my hair, then moved in closer to smell it.

"H-Hey, what are you…"

Ignoring her husband's words, she stroked my face, rubbed it, then squeezed it between her fingers. My smooth skin wasn't due to skin care products though; it was due to my youth, being in a fifteen-year-old's body. I didn't even use any skin care products in the first place. That stuff wasn't really needed until about age eighteen or so.

But there was no need to tell her such things, so I stayed quiet. It wasn't my fault she made the wrong assumption, and my skin care products were effective, so what was the harm?

"I will purchase them. Bring me a full set."

"H-Hey, shouldn't we…"

"Calamus, pay her."

"Yes, ma'am!"

"Hey…"

The transaction was done with the husband being completely ignored…

Shampoo, conditioner, skin lotion, serum, milky lotion, and some cream. Since they were for a noble, the products all came in artistic crystal glass containers. I even included a small bottle of perfume as a free bonus.

"That will be six small gold coins. The instructions on how to use them are written here. The amount and order of usage are listed there, so please be sure to follow them."

"Very well. I certainly hope they're effective, for the sake of your life…"

My, what a scary old lady!

But I'd succeeded in sowing the seeds for selling more skin care products. All I had to do now was wait for word of mouth to spread!

The nobles left without me even learning their names, and I thought it was about time to close shop for the day. But just as I was about to do so, two soldiers entered. They seemed to be a commissioned officer and a corporal.

"I'd like to purchase the soldier's disease medicine in bulk..."

Oh, here we go again...

I guess I'd have to deal with these types of people until the lieutenant colonel could get to all of them...

He must have been fast to act and quick-witted for someone of his rank to come here in person, and so soon, too... But he did end up saving me a great deal of trouble, so I guess I was thankful. I mean, he was doing it for his own merits and not out of the kindness of his heart. I guess it was what you'd call a mutually beneficial relationship.

Too bad these guys took the time to come here, when all they'd get was my rejection speech. I suppose I could at least sell them two bottles each, though. The lieutenant colonel's notice probably hadn't gotten around to them yet.

Now I can just look forward to more shampoo and cosmetics being sold and go on with running the business...

At that time, I hadn't realized...

There was no way a noblewoman would go around spreading the secret of how to preserve her beauty, and that this was clearly the type of secret she'd try to keep all for herself. The shampoos and cosmetic products didn't seem to be selling at all, and it took me quite some time to realize this.

Damn it!

*   *

"Hey, lady, want me to hold your groceries for you?"

A boy who seemed to be about seven or eight years old approached me on my way back from buying vegetables at the market. He may have been of a Western ethnicity, but he was still smaller than me, considering his age.

It was true that it was a bit tough carrying a massive quantity of food, especially radishes and cabbages, but this wasn't my first time doing it and it wasn't anything I couldn't handle. Using the Item Box would have made it a breeze, but I didn't intend on abusing it. I was concerned about being spotted using it, too.

The first time I went shopping at the market, Francette appeared out of nowhere and offered to carry my groceries, so I shooed her away in a fluster. A little girl making a knight carry her things would've stood out like a sore thumb. That would've been a surefire way to attract some unwanted attention.

Anyway… this boy surely wasn't offering out of the kindness of his heart.

"I'll do it for just two bronze coins!"

Yeah, thought so…

Two bronze coins would be about twenty yen. With the prices here, doing it three to four times would earn enough to buy one radish. That'd be enough food to feed a family of four, meaning four people would be able to live another day.

"All right, hired!"

"Thanks!"

I talked to the boy about various things on our way to my shop. Speaking to people of his status was quite interesting and offered valuable intel. They tended to tell it like it was without worrying unnecessarily about propriety and such.

"...That's why we don't really get to eat till we're full much of the time, so we're working to earn money, too!"

Our conversation had moved on to the boy's personal life. According to him, he lived at an orphanage. He wasn't belittling himself or trying to get some sympathy; he was just stating the simple facts. Even then, his words seemed to contain a sentiment like, "Someone as rich-looking as you probably has no idea what this life is like."

"An orphanage, huh... I have kids at my place who used to be orphans, too. Neither of them could get into an orphanage, so they lived in an abandoned building and nearly died a bunch of times because they didn't eat anything for days. Ahaha!"

"Wha..." The boy stopped walking.

"I'm all alone in this world, too, but I hired them to work for me... Why'd you stop walking? Is something wrong...?"

If you lived in an orphanage, you were already fortunate enough. Just as there were those with more in the world, there were also those with less. The slight differences in the starting point didn't end up being a big deal, in the end. This boy must've considered himself unfortunate for being an orphan which, to be fair, wasn't wrong.

However, there were countless people in the world who were less fortunate than him. The important thing to consider was, if they were unhappy one day, would they be unhappy the next? Would they be unhappy the day after that? What about ten years later? Twenty years?

It's not yet time to be flustered. Nor is it time for sorrow. That's all there was to it...

"Oh, we're here. This is my shop."

The boy seemed a little surprised as he saw Layette's Atelier. I gave him his two bronze coins, then he returned to the marketplace. He was probably going to go find his next customer. I prayed he'd continue on the righteous path instead of turning to pickpocketing like Emile and Belle used to do…

"Oh, Emile, could you make some deliveries with Belle for me tomorrow?"

"Yeah, sure. What do you need me to deliver, and where?"

Emile was finally learning not to instinctively speak to me in a formal manner, even when I talked to him out of nowhere. I was glad the distance between us seemed to be closing.

* *

The next day, they loaded up the cart they'd borrowed from a neighboring shop, and Emile and Belle departed from Layette's Atelier. Their destination was the orphanage Kaoru had heard about from the boy yesterday. The cart was loaded with some of the vast stockpile Kaoru had stored within her Item Box. Roland and Francette would sometimes hunt for rabbits, deer, or boar while they were camping, and whatever they caught was being kept within the box.

As soon as Emile and Belle arrived at their destination, they were surrounded by a large group of orphan children. It was still early, so it was before they'd gone out to try and earn some coin. It was also quite rare for outsiders, even young ones, to visit bringing such a huge quantity of food, which was why they'd come out in such numbers.

An aging woman, who seemed to be the director, and several other caretakers appeared in a fluster. Emile pointed at the cargo and stated, "These are from Lady Kaoru."

It wasn't an issue for him to address his employer as such. Every adult besides Kaoru, Roland, and Francette was an enemy. This was what Emile believed, and even if these people were there to help the orphans, he couldn't help that his speech became stiff when talking to them. He could compartmentalize speaking to those at the Hunters' Guild when he was working, but he ended up coming off as curt when it came to dealing with adult strangers like this.

"...Kaoru?"

"The person with the scary eyes," Belle cut in to reply to the director's question.

Then a boy's voice responded, "Oh, is she the one who hired me yesterday?"

"Yes, she did mention that she hired someone to carry her groceries from the marketplace."

"I knew it..."

The key phrase "scary eyes" was enough to identify Kaoru in all of the royal capital. It was extremely convenient.

At the same time, however, Belle and the boy were very rude to do so.

"So, Lady Kaoru instructed us to deliver this as a gift to all of you."

The children cheered in response to Belle's words, and began swarming all around the cart. The adults tried to stop them, but it was a futile effort.

A whole deer, horned rabbits, fruits, and more were taken from the cart. Cheap, bulky-looking vegetables and fish that were cheap due to having been bought at a coastal city had been omitted. It was mainly meat and fruits that they'd rarely be able to eat otherwise. The deer hadn't even had its intestines removed, but it was still as fresh as the day it was hunted due to being stored in the Item Box. Of course, this meant the intestines were also edible as well. There was no way the orphanage would throw out some perfectly good, fresh intestines.

"Oooooohhh!"

A deer! Not a monster like an orc or forest wolf, but an actual deer! Even the adults raised their voices in admiration. That was just how great a feast that a deer would be.

They could purchase five kilograms of orc meat rather than one kilogram of deer meat for the same price. This went without saying. This was why deer meat would never be served at the orphanage; there was just no way.

"Everyone, it's time for a song! A song and dance of appreciation for the Goddess Celestine!" the director called out, then the children surrounded the cart and began performing a strange dance.

And so, the orphanage was in a state of chaos.

"...I want to go home," Emile muttered, at a loss for what to do.

Belle nodded in agreement, but they still had to return the cart they had borrowed. To do that, they had to wait for the dance to finish...

The two just stood there, and eventually one of the boys spoke up.

"Is it true you two were orphans?"

It was the boy Kaoru had hired.

"...Yes. Belle and I were orphans when we were young. An orphanage would have been a paradise compared to how we grew up. There were seven of us, crawling on the ground and licking mud, just barely managing to survive, like insects… Every year, more would join us, and every year, several of us would die. That's what our life was like. That is, until the day we met Lady Kaoru…"

Emile looked off into the distance.

"Please tell me! How did you manage it? How did you become a full-fledged hunter with such impressive equipment so quickly as an orphan? How did an orphan like Kaoru end up owning a shop like that?!"

Before he knew it, the singing had stopped, and the other children were surrounding Emile and Belle.

So many eyes, staring right at him…

H-Help me, Belle!

Emile turned around to find Belle had quietly stepped away to put more distance between them.

"Bellllle!"

And so, Emile desperately tried to provide an explanation that made sense, while maintaining that Kaoru was just an ordinary girl. It was certainly difficult to explain Kaoru's story without her goddess powers or her title as an angel.

Lady Kaoru, I'm sorryyy!

*　　*

It had been five days since I made a deal with Lieutenant Colonel Vonsas to deliver medicine for him. It was about time for me to tell him that I'd received my bulk order from my "manufacturer," so I decided to go and deliver the medicine. I'd already paid an orphan child to carry my message, so the appointment was set.

It was common to hire orphan children as messengers, and they wouldn't possibly do a halfhearted job and thus risk the reputation of their orphanage. This much was obvious, considering no one would trust orphans with such jobs in the future if their reputation was tarnished. That's why orphan messengers were much more reliable than asking some random adult to do it.

Besides, I was used to asking orphans to complete jobs for me. I'd done so with the children of the Eyes of the Goddess.

Now that I thought about it, Emile and Belle were orphans, too. They couldn't get into an orphanage, had no food, couldn't get medicine when they got sick, had lice, and were uncertain whether or not they'd live to see the next day. Though, that was hard to imagine now…

But ever since I'd sent those two to the orphanage, the orphans had sure taken a liking to me… I'd occasionally send them food, so maybe they appreciated me as a sponsor or a patron, or some other kind of generous supporter. There were usually some orphans on standby in front of my place, but there had to be a better place for them than that…

Moreover, the gate guards wouldn't turn away orphan messengers. They were aware that those children would take on such jobs, and some soldiers used to be orphans themselves. There were even some soldiers' orphans. Very few soldiers mistreated them for that very reason.

In any case, the arrival of my delivery had been communicated to them already. I was also bringing Layette with me of course. This was part of my plan to get recognized by some soldiers so they'd help me later, so there was no reason not to bring her.

Yes, the idea was to make them think that Layette and I had to be protected if they didn't want their supply of medicine cut off. Even if Layette wasn't directly involved in the creation of the medicine, if I ever caught wind of a soldier seeing her in trouble but ignoring it…

I was going to make sure the lieutenant colonel knew what I'd think if such a thing ever happened. Oh yes, I'd tell him in great detail.

Now, the problem was the quantity of medicine to be delivered. It would be suspicious if I brought too much, and he'd complain if I brought too little. Striking the right balance was the difficult part.

I'd only be delivering the medicine priced at three silver coins and three small gold coins. He thought I was losing money on the small-silver treatments , and it'd be a problem if I gave the army medicine that only prevented the issue from getting worse instead of curing it.

It took about a month for the three-silver treatments to cure the condition, while the three small gold ones took about five days. The amount of time differed based on various factors, such as the degree of the condition upon starting the treatment, the user's body chemistry, and the method of application. In terms of amount, it required about forty applications for the toes on both feet. I overestimated the amount so as to make sure it'd be cured with one bottle.

However, the silver one could require more than a bottle if the condition spread further than the toes or if the medicine was applied poorly. This was part of the reason why I limited purchases to two bottles per person. The silver one should've been enough for one person a bottle, and the small-gold one should've been enough for about eight people per bottle. Although it was ten times the price, it could be used on eight times the people and took less time to cure the condition, so I thought it was pretty fair.

For the first delivery, I settled on seventy-two bottles of the small-gold, and twenty-four bottles of the silver. Each box contained twenty-four bottles, with four boxes in all. Doing the math, 72 x 8 + 24 equaled 600 people total. Ten deliveries would provide treatment for 6,000 people. I doubted every soldier needed treatment, so they probably wouldn't need that many.

Yeah, that should do it.

Once most of them were cured, I'd sell some more to anyone with recurring symptoms.

...Wait, my sales for this batch will be twenty-two gold coins, three small gold coins and two silver coins? Whaaa?!

I need to open a bank account... Wait, there's no such thing here! I'll go to the Merchants' Guild... Wait, what about my Item Box? C-Calm down, me!

The reason I was bringing more of the small-gold one was because I wanted to decrease the number of patients as soon as possible, considering there were so many of them. Sure, it was important to make it seem like I needed stock for retail sales, but I was prioritizing the army with the good stuff.

Okay, let's go!

I held hands with Layette and began walking toward the army barracks, located near the northern gate of the royal capital. The military-related buildings and facilities were located on the inner side of the outer walls, but the training grounds, which required much more space, were located outside. I mean, if there was ever conflict, there might be a siege, so it only made sense to have military facilities inside the walls. In that case, they'd go directly outside from the northern gate instead of through the city, but if they weren't short on time or if they wanted to increase morale, they'd march through the city and out the southern gate.

Hm, I guess they do bother to use their brains...

I put twenty-four bottles in each of the four boxes, then put two boxes each into a pair of bags, with one bag on each shoulder.

Uuugh, so heavy...

Roland and Francette followed from behind, pretending not to know me. I think they were worrying a bit too much, personally. It was still morning, we were walking in the middle of the main road, and I was heading to the army headquarters. You couldn't really get much safer than that.

How was I supposed to have privacy if they always worried about me and followed me everywhere I went? I wouldn't even be able to go on a date in peace. Not that I had anyone to go on a date with...

When I arrived at the main gate, they let me pass through right away. It seemed they were forewarned of my arrival, as there was actually a guide waiting for us there. Though, really, I guess they couldn't just have us wandering around without knowing where to go, and it wasn't like we could use a phone to call someone over, which explained why someone was waiting for us. I guess that much was to be expected of a capable lieutenant colonel who had outperformed all his colleagues.

Roland and Francette couldn't follow me inside, so their secret send-off ended here. Now they could go on a date or something.

...They wouldn't be waiting for me until I was done, would they? I mean, I already told them I might take a while, since this was my first visit and I'd probably be speaking to the person in charge of ordering, and I might even take a look around, so I doubted they would...

I was taken to a room with a nameplate on the door: "Second Battalion Commander."

...I thought I was being taken to the person in charge here!

Well, we were dealing with important strategic goods (for his soldiers), so maybe he was being cautious about reselling and pilfering.

"Welcome."

I was seeing Lieutenant Colonel Vonsas for the first time in five days. He was all smiles and seemed to be in a good mood.

"Because of you, I was able to settle various issues and conflicts with other battalions. I thank you."

Huh...

The bags were heavy, so I took out the medicine boxes and placed them on the visitors' table. I put one of the now-empty bags into the other bag, along with the emptied medicine box.

"Three boxes of seventy-two bottles worth three small gold coins each. One box of twenty-four bottles worth three silver coins each. The total comes to twenty-two gold coins, three small gold coins, and two silver coins."

"Very well. Here."

The soldier who guided me there brought out a small cloth bag from the lieutenant colonel's desk.

The quantity and price had already been conveyed in a letter that had been delivered by the messenger from the orphanage. This was common courtesy as a working adult. It would've been troublesome if I had requested such a large amount to be paid up front, in cash, on the spot.

I pretended to put the cloth money bag in my own bag, but put it inside my Item Box. A capable woman doesn't walk around carelessly with such a huge sum of money.

"I've put out a notice to go through me for any inquiries about the medicine. I presume there haven't been any issues at your shop?"

"No, thanks to you..."

There had been several soldiers coming in for medicine for two or three days since that day, but I was able to handle anyone asking for bulk purchases on their superior's orders with the lieutenant colonel's authority. I treated any soldier who didn't know about the circumstances as a normal customer, so there hadn't been any issues.

"Well, then, I'll be looking forward to the future deliveries. Do you have any requests from your end?" he said with courtesy, perhaps because we were children.

Maybe he was just saying it for the sake of politeness, but he had committed by saying it, so I was going to take advantage of it, because that's how I roll!

"Then, please show me around! I may come back to deliver medicine somewhere else here, and I find these places interesting!"

Yeah, that wasn't a lie. My earnings with the soldier's disease medicine would probably slow down in about two months, so I wanted to scope out the area to search for other potential business opportunities. I could also accomplish my original goal to get recognized and look for handsome men at the same time.

That's right, I'm a go-getter!

Though it wasn't as if I was desperate or anything.

No, really.

"Let's go, then," the lieutenant colonel said, rising.

You're gonna show me around? Not your subordinate?!

"Well, I'm just glad such a cute young lady has interest in the workings of the military."

Really? I had a feeling there was more to it…

In any case, the lieutenant colonel showed us around the property as per his suggestion. We had a sort of placard displayed on our chests and backs as we walked around. I'd written the following on the signs the previous night:

"Medicine Shop - Layette's Atelier."

This was to show everyone that the medicine for soldier's disease was being supplied by our shop. This was half the reason I was there making deliveries in the first place.

We were the center of attention! It was customary for everyone to look and salute as soon as the lieutenant colonel appeared. There was an even greater visual impact with little girls like Layette and myself next to him, along with the signs. How could we not attract attention?

I wasn't sure if the lieutenant colonel knew what I was up to, or just thought I was advertising my shop… But in any case, we succeeded in imprinting in the minds of the royal army's soldiers that if something were to happen to us two, their beacon of hope, the soldier's disease medicine would no longer be attainable.

*   *

After the lieutenant colonel showed us around, he brought us to the mess hall. It was a military mess hall, so it wasn't open around the clock or anything. They only served food during the soldiers' meal times for breakfast, lunch, and dinner. Any other time, they just prepped and ordered food, cleaned equipment, and handled office work, so they never just sat around bored. But those sorts of tasks were all done in the kitchens or offices instead of at the food storage area, so there was no one at the mess hall at the moment.

"This is the mess hall for corporals and the lower ranks. Officers have a separate mess hall of their own. Though, company commanders and higher take their food to their rooms unless we're having a group meal together."

"Hmm. So, that way, the higher-ups won't all go down at once if there's a disease going around or the food gets poisoned…"

"Huh?"

The lieutenant colonel seemed a bit surprised. Maybe that wasn't why it was set up that way after all.

"We sell medicine for illnesses and antidotes, too, just so you know."

"R-Right…" He seemed to be a bit taken aback.

Huh. Maybe, in this world, they didn't do things like sneaking into enemy posts to poison their wells or chop up plague-infested corpses and launch them into enemy territory with catapults during a siege. Those were common tactics back on Earth…

Oh, there are some things posted on the board.

"I will be purchasing the soldier's disease medicine in bulk. Soldiers are to refrain from visiting the retailer of their own accord, and must receive treatment at the infirmary."

Huh, this must be the notice the lieutenant colonel put out for me…

There were various other pieces of paper pinned to the board, like a recruitment notice for the swordsmanship society or a puppy needing a home.

I'd seen these sorts of notices on the board at my company's food court too. It seemed it was the same wherever you went.

Next, he took us to the outdoor training grounds, where soldiers were busy doing drills. Apparently, the large-scale military exercises were done on the spacious maneuvering ground outside the city gates, or they did marching drills on their way to a location some distance away to train there.

I looked over next to the training grounds and saw a small group of people operating what seemed to be some sort of box. The lieutenant colonel explained when he saw me watching with curiosity.

"Ah, that's communication training. That box contains hand flags during the day and candles at night, and the front can be opened and closed to send out signals. It's still daytime, so they're practicing with red cloth instead of candles."

Huh, so they had flag and flash signals here. Sort of like Morse code.

"I can read them, to a degree, but I never officially trained for it, and I can't read anything when they signal that quickly. Though, I wouldn't need to send signals myself in my position, so I can just take my time, should the need ever arise. I say leave the signaling to the signalers and cooking to the cooks."

Yeah, he had a point. Higher-ups should leave tasks to whoever's in charge of them instead of butting in every time. My sales manager badly needed to learn that...

Uh, never mind. That was all in the past...

"Huh? What's that?" I noticed them making signals for us. "'Who are they'... 'Medicine shop sisters'... 'Why are they here'... 'To come see me'... 'The little one is mine'... Do you mind if I go punch them in the head?"

"...How are you able to read that? But, yes, I'll allow it."

"Ah..."

Yes, it was because of "that": The ability to speak, read, and write any language.

Their Morse code counts as a language too?!

"..."

"..."

"..."

"..."

"...So, that's about everything there is to see at this base."

Yes, I won! I ran over to the signalers and kicked them.

But this was considered a "base," huh... Even though it was part of the royal capital?

Speaking of which, there were naval and air bases, while the army had garrisons. Maybe it was like how ships and planes couldn't operate without a home base, but the army could go anywhere, so long as they had supplies, so "base" just meant where they were currently and was used interchangeably with "post."

Though, unlike the navy or air force, which deployed out of their base every time, the army didn't necessarily return every time they went out, so maybe it wasn't a "base" in that sense. Maybe because the royal army didn't tend to fight outside the kingdom from one battle to another, the place they were stationed at was considered their base.

As I had completed my goals and returned to my shop, there was no way for me to know...

A rumor had been going around between the soldiers that "the older sister from the potion shop with the mean eyes provided great services by kicking you"...

* *

Three days later…

"I would like to purchase the soldier's disease medicine in bulk."

A somewhat elderly, officer-looking man arrived at the shop. This was odd, seeing as the lieutenant colonel should've told him about our arrangement…

"Um, about that… The royal army's second battalion commander, Lieutenant Colonel Vonsas, should've…"

But the man scowled, and basically spit out his next words.

"'The royal army's second battalion commander, Lieutenant Colonel Vonsas…' That man monopolized all the medicine for the royal army and hasn't supplied the guard regiment with a single bottle! But when my men come here, they're told to contact him instead… You must do something. If you don't, there will be conflict between the guards and the royal army! We work as security at the royal palace, we provide protection for nobles, and we serve as the honor guard for major ceremonies, so we cannot just scratch freely like the royal army can! Why do you give them favorable treatment and give us nothing?!"

Ahhh, that was unfortunate…

Lieutenant Colonel, you've only been giving it to your own men?!

But, well, I supposed there'd be no potential gain in him providing it for other organizations…

However, I couldn't just let this pass. Even though I hadn't known about the guard regiment, this was pretty horrible.

"Very well. My next delivery will be sent to the guard regiment. How many guards are there?"

"Ah! Ahhh! That's fantastic! Thank you, I truly appreciate it! Due to our station, there aren't very many of us. There are four platoons, headquarters, support personnel—all together, about 200 men."

According to the officer, who was apparently a captain of the guard regiment, the transportation units and such who accompanied the royal family on their foreign travels came from other teams, and weren't on the scale of a standard company. Perhaps the lieutenant colonel was ignoring them because of their small size, or maybe they simply didn't get along.

Well, 200 or so didn't sound like a problem. It would only take twenty-five bottles of the medicine worth three small gold coins. I doubted every one of them had the condition, but a box of twenty-four should be more than enough.

It was a bit odd that this man was a captain leading a platoon though. Platoons were usually led by a second or first lieutenant, so maybe the ranks were inflated in the guard regiment. Oh, but if they made the top rank of the guard regiment a captain or major, it would cause major problems within their power structure! I guessed it just ended up that way when they assigned ranks from the top without considering the number of men.

"I actually have one more request, though it's a bit hard to bring up, considering you just granted me a favor..."

"Oh? What is it?" He seemed hesitant, but I decided to hear him out.

"I was hoping you could supply your medicine to the royal sentries, as well..."

What?! The sentries were basically like police officers on Earth, and kept the peace at the royal capital. Their daily work consisted of mock training, and unlike the royal army, who could earn accolades and promotions for their performance, every day was a battle on the job for them. They had to deal with criminals and drunk soldiers, or hunters swinging swords around, and certainly didn't get praise or treated like heroes for facing such dangers and capturing criminals.

Was he saying these people weren't getting any of the medicine either? I messed up! Because of my ignorance, I thought the soldiers of all the different branches were just soldiers, and didn't consider how they could all be considered parts of separate entities. This captain was even considering organizations other than his own, but that lieutenant colonel...

Oh, I got it. A "capable" person was the type who was good at making profits for themselves. This, in turn, meant keeping others from benefiting, as well. But just how far did this notion apply? I'd need to be careful, too...

"Very well. It seems I've been trusting the royal army a little too much. Please tell the sentries to send someone over my way."

They probably had already, and I must've sent them away to contact Lieutenant Colonel Vonsas. So, they must've come by individually, but I'd been limiting daily sales to avoid suspicion, so it was probably sold out by the time they visited after work.

I felt bad... Though, really, I chose to sell the type of medicine nobles and rich people would be interested in instead of the type that cured injuries or illnesses to avoid this sort of trouble, so why was I dealing with this now? Was soldier's disease that horrible a condition?

...Yeah, it probably was.

Damn it. I guess I'll increase my numbers for general sales.

...Sales for my other medicines weren't doing so well. And why weren't my shampoo, conditioner, and other cosmetics selling? I wondered if that noble wife was actually advertising for me...

*　　*

"Hey, lady, want me to hold your stuff?"

After I finished shopping at the marketplace and began heading back to the shop, a voice called to me. An orphan child had offered to help me every time, as of late. Guess I was sort of a regular.

"Yeah, if you don't mi… Huh?"

It was an unfamiliar face. I wasn't good at memorizing people's faces, so it wasn't like I knew what all the orphans looked like, but it was usually the same few kids who went to the marketplace to find work. This one looked more ragged than the children from the orphanage, too…

I thought about this idly as I started handing over my bags, when…

"Hey, what are you doing?!" It was the usual boy. "Kaoru is ours! Don't even think about it!"

Huh? Since when did I belong to the orphanage?

Oh… So this was a competitor. Did that mean this child wasn't from the orphanage?

"You're from the riverbank, aren't you? You can do business here, but you aren't touching Kaoru!"

"What? It's none of your business who I work for! I'm putting my life on the line out here. I don't have it easy and get spoon-fed two meals a day like you!"

Huh… If he thought an orphanage child had it easy, there was only one explanation; those who thought even kids in an orphanage were wealthy and blessed.

A street urchin.

"Whoever's faster and provides the better offer wins. That's business. So, how much?"

"Two bronze coins."

I guess the rate was the same, as expected.

"Okay then, deal."

I handed my bags to the street urchin child, and the boy from the orphanage watched with a dumbfounded expression.

"Huh...?"

There was a look of disbelief and betrayal in his eyes, but... it's not like I owed him anything.

As we walked together, I began gathering more information, as per usual. Of course, the children at the orphanage weren't the only orphans in the royal capital in a world like this. I should've known that after seeing everyone at the Eyes of the Goddess. At the very least, the orphanage kids wouldn't be starving to death. These street urchins were a different story, since there was no one here to help them.

"I have a former street urchin at my place, too. He's working under me as a guard now."

"Huh...?"

"Emile, Belle, I need you to get the cart for me again. We're going out with it tomorrow."

"Huh...?"

Emile and Belle would do anything to protect Kaoru. They'd memorized all the faces of the children at the orphanage, thinking they could be useful as a shield for Kaoru, should the need ever arise.

But the boy who had been carrying her bags earlier was unfamiliar, and his clothes should've been a bit more presentable if he was actually from that facility.

They had a bad feeling about this…

The next day…

The three of them packed supplies onto the cart and headed toward the riverbank. Kaoru was also there this time, assuming there'd be no cooking tools or seasoning available.

And so…

"You guys used to be street urchins?"

"Y-Yeah…"

"How did you earn such nice equipment so quickly?"

"W-Well…"

Emile turned around to find Belle had already backed some distance away.

A few days later…

When Kaoru went shopping at the marketplace, numerous children were following her closely. They were divided in two groups and glaring at each other behind her…

"Gimme a breeeak!!!"

Chapter 24: The Noble Returns

Finally, goods other than the soldier's disease medicine began selling. But the shampoo and cosmetics? Nuh-uh.

...Why?!

Instead, I'd been selling items that could be appraised for their quality just by looking at them: Glassware and ceramics.

For glassware, I'd been using crystal glass, which was clearly higher quality than other glass in this time period, despite having the transparency reduced quite a bit. As for ceramics, I sold imitation maiolica and Otani ware as my crockery, and imitation Imari ware and Kutani ware as my porcelains.

I actually liked pottery, so I knew about clays, glazes, and firing temperatures to make them. I'd seen many of these types at exhibits and had handled them in person myself. Even though I wouldn't be able to fire them up myself, I had no problem "ordering" them from the goddess's manufacturing factory.

I felt a little guilty about stealing designs from famous artistic pieces, but no one could really blame me for paying homage to the genre of "x ware." Though, I did make sure to be extra careful not to soil the name of the original work, of course.

One thing that had been on my mind was that I suspected people may be reselling my products.

Yes, I know. Buying low and selling high were the absolute basics of business. The buyers were able to find out about products they couldn't have otherwise thanks to the middleman, and they paid the fee that they found most reasonable.

Creator, buyer, seller… It was a legitimate economic activity that made everyone happy.

…Screw that!

I absolutely despised resellers. Ever since the day I was a second too late in clicking "buy" to get some concert tickets and I saw the same ticket being resold online for five times the price!

There must be a way to punish those horrid resellers…

Clang…

"Hmm, so this is the place…"

I was deep in thought when a sketchy-looking group entered the shop. One noble, one servant-looking person, three guards, and the realtor who had leased this shop to me.

Ahhh, I smell trouble again…

"Welcome!"

"Well-ell-cooome!"

There was Layette's super-stuttered greeting, a running gag at the shop. She must have been feeling obligated to do it now or something… She may succeed in observing neutrinos, at this rate.

But, once again, I missed my chance to have Layette take cover upstairs. I needed to think of a better method to prevent these situations. Maybe I'd make an ejection seat that could let her escape with a push of a button… Actually, she'd just hit the ceiling and break her neck doing that.

"I am not a customer. I'm the owner of this shop, Count Oram."

"Huh?"

I'd rented the shop from a realtor, and heard it used to be a general store owned by an old couple. But I'd also heard they'd closed shop because their children hadn't wanted to keep the business going, and so they'd rented it out to use that income to retire. It shouldn't have belonged to any noble. I wouldn't have rented it if it was connected to nobles in the first place.

I looked at the realtor, who seemed rather apologetic…

"Don't worry, I don't plan on kicking you out or anything of the sort. But since the owner has changed, the previous contract is now void. You will need to sign a new contract with me, so I took my time to come here in person. Bring out the contract."

"Yes, sir!" The servant-looking person next to him produced documents from a leather bag and presented them to me. I took them and began skimming through…

Henceforth, the lessor will be referred to as "A" and the lessee will be referred to as "B."

B is to make payments to A worth half of this store's earnings as part of rental expenses.

B is to obey A's designations on pricing of the products sold at this store.

B is to obey A's directions regarding which buyers products from this store will be sold to.

B is to disclose any and all information regarding the suppliers and manufacturing methods of products sold at this store.

B is to…

Haha.

Hahahaha.

Ahahahaha!

…What sort of bad joke is this?

"Excuse me, but 60% of the cost goes into purchasing materials, 20% into expenses for processing the products here, and then we're left with a 20% profit. With these terms, we would lose more money the more we sell…"

"Then you only need to raise your prices. Simply double your prices to keep the same profits, and triple them to increase them even further. Use your brain!"

Oof! I couldn't believe I was just told to use my brain by someone like him!

…Fine. Use my brain, you say? Okay, then.

"Very well. Then let us sign the contract. There must be two copies, correct?"

"Y-Yes, of course…"

Count Oram seemed a bit taken aback that I agreed to the contract so quickly. The realtor had a similar look on his face. I mean, no one would normally agree to such a ridiculous contract. Maybe he thought a little girl couldn't possibly oppose a noble, so he looked down on me with a look of pity and apathy.

After some time, the contracts were signed and we went over the various terms. The count left with a satisfied look. I figured he wasn't just after half of the earnings, but wanted to control the sales of the soldier's disease medicine, glassware, and ceramics that had been gaining popularity, and seize the political clout that'd come with them.

As a count, he was about the same social standing as the lieutenant colonel's family, who was only the third son, with a low chance of inheriting the title. On the other hand, the count was the head of the family himself. The difference in standing between the head and a third son was obvious, and since he was unaffiliated with the military, he had no reason to listen to the lieutenant colonel's orders. In fact, there'd be a big problem if a soldier tried to give orders to a noble.

Military personnel were nobles themselves, but they couldn't give orders to someone with a higher standing. He must have heard about our shop and leapt at the chance to gain more standing.

A noble who wasn't a serviceman would likely have a servant wash and apply scented oils to their feet, so he likely didn't have soldier's disease himself.

In any case, he'd done it now. Yeah, I was pretttttty harsh with those who opposed me so maliciously.

"Please explain," I said to the realtor after the count and his crew left.

"I apologize… Though, to be fair, we haven't made any mistakes on our end, so I hope you do understand that."

With that preamble, the realtor explained the situation. The count's messenger had appeared at the realtor's place yesterday, claiming that he'd purchased this shop. He requested that the realtor arrange a meeting with the new lessee to sign a new contract. Taken by complete surprise, the realtor quickly checked with the old couple who owned the store, who explained that they were asked to sell the property with an offer higher than market price. They didn't want to get on the bad side of a noble, and the terms weren't bad, so they agreed to sell it.

Such were the circumstances. The owner had changed, so I had no choice but to agree to the lending terms proposed by them.

"Therefore, we had little choice in the matter… I'm very sorry the terms have changed from the previous contract, but if you don't agree to it, you will need to leave. In fact, that's what I thought you would have done…"

Yeah, he must've been quite confused when I agreed to those terms. I mean, if I were to find another store for rent, modify the interior, and move everything, it'd take so much time and money, and I would have to put a pause on business for some time.

...Normally, of course. Usually, one would prefer that to agreeing to such ludicrous terms.

...Yeah, usually.

But as soon as I reopened my business, that noble would appear again, saying he was the new owner of that shop, too. And so, I brought up an idea to the apologetic-looking realtor.

"Um, I have a sort of request..."

Women and merchants couldn't let people walk all over them.

Behold the wrath of the Nagase clan!

*　*

"Hmm, I suppose it's time to go retrieve the products from that shop..."

First thing in the morning, Count Oram decided to visit the medicine shop he'd basically acquired whole. He was a bit hesitant to do anything immediately after making the agreement, so he'd left after signing the contract yesterday, but he had no intention of leaving it alone for too long.

First, he'd take any product that seemed useful to him. He'd instruct the girl not to sell those products to anyone else, but to set them at a low price. The prices for everything else would be hiked up, then he'd reap half the sales.

The sales of a small shop such as this were hardly significant to someone of his station. However, the reason he acquired that store wasn't for such petty earnings. The goal was to obtain the shop and every product being sold there.

All of it.

The supply route for the materials, manufacturing methods, methods of obtaining the glassware and ceramics—everything. And he wasn't reluctant to the idea of taking care of that shopkeeper either. She was quite young, but that wasn't in opposition to his tastes.

Should be any minute now…

"We've arrived, sir."

With the servant's call, the guards who had been accompanying him got off first and checked their surroundings for any danger. The count then descended the steps that had been prepared for him and slowly got off the carriage. When he opened the door to the medicine shop…

"Welcome!"

Two well-spoken and synchronized voices greeted him.

"Huh…?" The count's eyes widened.

…They were gone. The product shelves lining the walls, the medicine bottles, glasswork, ceramics, and indescribable miscellaneous goods—all of them. The emptied shop only had one table, with what seemed to be some box lunches on the table. At the register was a young man, who seemed to be about sixteen or seventeen years old, and a girl of eleven or twelve. The shopkeeper girl and her younger sister were nowhere in sight.

"Wha…"

Count Oram was dumbfounded. He was frozen for ten whole seconds, then began shouting at the young man.

"Wh-Wh-What's the meaning of this?! Where're the medicine and ceramics? Where are those damn sisters?!"

He hurried over to the counter and leaned in, spitting and shouting. Emile leaned away from him and began explaining.

"Oh, our manager? She's at the shop."

"Where?! I don't see her anywhere!" the count exclaimed.

Emile seemed to realize the issue, then began explaining in detail, "No, she's at the branch store. Since she's bleeding money here and has to keep her agreement with her suppliers about their private information, she said we'll only sell items here that she doesn't mind disclosing how to make. So, now we're selling those meals over there. We make boxed lunches in the morning to sell to hunters and craftsmen. After some time, we'll close up shop and head to work ourselves. We sell thirty meals for three small silver coins each, which comes to ninety small silver coins. We do this twenty days a month, for a total of eighteen small gold coins. Half of it goes to rent, so that's about nine small coins a month, which sounds about adequate. Though, that is if we sell out every day… So, starting today, this store will be a warehouse-slash-residence-slash-box-lunch-shop, and the medicine shop has been moved to the branch store."

"Wh-Wh-Whaaaaaat?!"

Indeed, Kaoru had a stern word with the realtor and demanded that he find an open shop that could be rented out right away. The realtor had tried to claim that he wasn't responsible, but she wasn't going to take that for an answer. She pulled out the original contract from the Item Box and repeatedly read the terms, told him what happened to businesses that lost the trust of their clients, and managed to at least get him to find her a temporary shop.

All on the same day.

Of course, she had no intention of doing business there permanently, so she wasn't as picky as she had been with choosing the main branch. She just needed some place that could be used right away. She'd rented it out for the irregular terms of no deposit and no rent for the first week, and thus Layette's Atelier Mk-II was created.

It was called the "branch store" or "second store" externally, but in her mind it was "Mk-II." She had quite a hard time deciding between naming it "G" or "Mk-II."

Count Oram made a scene, demanding to be taken to the branch store, so Emile showed him the way. Even if they'd ignored him, he'd eventually find it quite easily. In that case, it was better to take him there already, while Emile was still around. That was the thought process for Emile's decision.

"You watch the shop, Belle. Kaoru would cry if we left too many unsold meals on the first day."

Indeed, these meals had been handmade by Kaoru and Belle, instead of being created as potions. Of course, it would have been possible for Kaoru to use her ability to create any medicine with the effect she wanted them to have to make them appear in an instant.

She usually called them "potions," but it was actually the power to create medicine, and wasn't limited to fluids. If it contained even a little bit of water or other fluid it could be classified as a potion, but it wasn't a prerequisite. It could create solids without any issues whatsoever.

But Kaoru thought that wasn't quite right. She didn't mind creating "medicine" that was like a box lunch if she were hungry, of course, but the idea of creating medicine with her powers and selling it as a meal went against her personal policy. That was something Kaoru just couldn't bring herself to do, and she had no intention of changing this.

"...Fine."

Although Emile might soon end up in a dangerous situation, Belle waved him off without any deep display of emotion.

It wasn't that she didn't care. If this was some other situation, Belle would've stopped Emile or would have insisted on going with him.

But this was related to Kaoru's safety. She wasn't much of a fighter, and she'd only take out one or two people with her hidden knife at best. Or she'd be taken as a hostage and just make the situation worse. In that case, it was better for her to protect Kaoru's sanctuary. If Emile fell, she'd take vengeance by ambushing their enemies and become Kaoru's shield in his stead, continuing to protect her by the Goddess Celestine's blessing until the day they met again.

This was Belle's form of loyalty.

In addition, she couldn't get in the way of Emile carrying out his duty and his own act of loyalty. After all, they'd been saved by the Goddess and pledged their devotion to her as members of the Eyes of the Goddess.

Completely oblivious to Belle's intense determination, Kaoru was tending Layette's Atelier Mk-II, with Layette sitting on her lap.

* *

Clang...

"Welcome!"

"Well-ell-cooome!"

Layette, I think that could almost be considered a theatrical performance.

"Emile? What are you doing here...? Wait, Count Whatshisname?"

"Count Oram! Girl, why have you done such a..."

"Of course I was going to retaliate when you imposed unreasonable terms on me and demanded my money, products, and secrets. I'm not stupid."

"Wh-What…?"

The count had a surprised look on his face, but was that really so shocking?

"I haven't broken any promises and have done just as the contract stipulates. I just need to turn in half my earnings from the box lunch sales every week, correct?" I asked nonchalantly, and the count's face turned bright red.

"Wh-What nonsense is this? Do you realize what will happen if you anger me by keeping up this foolishness?!"

"Nothing, I'd guess?"

"What?!"

No, I really didn't think anything would come of it.

"If you try buying this building again, I'll just move somewhere else. For my next location, I could ask to use the lieutenant colonel's family connections, or, if need be, rent out a room on military property and use it as a post exchange."

I also had the option of renting out a stall as a mobile shop, but there was no need to play that card just yet. Count Oram likely assumed that transferring shops would take far too much time and energy for it to be worth the trouble. But, seeing how easily I had moved everything out in one night, he should've realized he had the wrong idea.

"Ugh, urrrgh…"

Military, nobility, and business were all separate. But the lieutenant colonel's father, a count, would likely need to save face if some other noble disrespected him by interfering with the store his son was doing business with. If word of this got out, it'd become apparent who the malefactor was here.

In the world of the nobility, which put heavy emphasis on honor and appearances, this would be rather inconvenient for Count Oram. Besides, he'd be completely unable to do anything if I were to move my shop to military territory. The only thing that'd be left was the incredible dishonor he'd incur trying such an outlandish and ridiculous move, then being easily outmaneuvered by a little girl, and a commoner at that.

"If I really have to, I'll just close up shop and move to another country. It's not like I was born here, so I don't have to stay here by any means. All I'd have to do is reopen my shop somewhere else. And before I move, I'll be sure to let the townspeople, Lieutenant Colonel Vonsas, the royal army, the guard regiment, and the sentries know that I'm moving because I couldn't stand Count Oram's unreasonable demands. It'd be rude to close down without stating my reasons, after all."

The count fell silent, his face completely red. If that happened, word would spread throughout the royal capital, and he'd make enemies out of the royal army, the guard regiment, and the sentries.

The military had many connections, from the head of the noble families to their children, and many, many more besides. Of course, this included merchants, as well. Count Oram had tried to take control of the soldier's disease medicine to build relationships with these merchants, but this incident would turn them into enemies, instead. This would be a fatal blow for a noble, not only for himself, but for his family and their entire faction. In fact, his faction would likely cut ties with him immediately, out of fear of becoming directly associated with the whole ordeal.

Should I have been making such aggressive moves against a noble? Well, this country was quite proper, and even nobles couldn't bring harm to a commoner for the sole purpose of monetary gain. If such a practice was to be accepted, it'd be impossible to do business with the nobility, as every rich merchant would just get hit up for their wealth. This would ruin the kingdom's entire economy.

But what if he lost his temper from being mocked by a little girl and ordered his guards to murder me? Well, Francette and Roland saw Emile come in with the noble and his guards, so they'd been positioned to draw their swords and attack ever since. They were acting like normal customers, but even an amateur like me could tell they were focusing all their senses on watching the guards for any hostile movements.

The bodyguards likely knew this too. They'd been sweating profusely for a while now.

It seemed that Count Oram wasn't going to make any stupid moves and instead just decided to give up. The guards seemed rather relieved once they knew that he was going to withdraw quietly. I guess people past a certain level could tell by their aura or something that some people shouldn't be messed with.

"Damn, I took that girl too lightly! I suppose pushing any further would only tarnish my reputation..."

The count seemed to understand when it was time to fold. As with most matters, it was much more difficult, and much more important, to know when to withdraw than when to move forward.

Many couldn't stand to lose the funds they'd already invested or hoped for a shot at a big comeback, and thus only made their losses worse by not admitting their failure. But the count, at least, had some sense in him.

"I will sell your shop back. It's too much trouble to keep that property for the petty sales from boxed meals. It would only lose me money. I don't need strange rumors going around about me, either… Though, I don't know how many people you've hired to pull off such a feat… I won't bother you any further, so return to your original location and, uh… you should make sure false rumors don't start spreading. Right."

Ah, so he was putting up the white flag and asking for mercy. I supposed I'd comply, then.

"Very well. And you wouldn't be selling it back for a higher price, would you? It would be common courtesy to offer a very low price, considering the inconvenience you've created for everyone from your unreasonable actions and demands."

"Ugh… O-Of course. Naturally, that goes without saying…"

He seemed rather bitter, but reluctantly agreed. I doubted he'd be lowering the price too much, but I wanted to let the old couple, who were happy about selling it for a high price, and the realtor, who went through all that guilt, to get something out of all this.

Count Oram left soon after. I had Emile return to the main store right away. Belle was likely worried, so I didn't want to leave her wondering as to what exactly was going on.

I then asked the realtor to come by the branch store that afternoon. The count had said that he'd go see the realtor directly, so I wanted to ask after the results. I couldn't begin moving again without confirmation, and I wanted to know how the conversation had gone.

It was unlikely he'd try something at this point, but there was the possibility of the realtor trying to come out on top after all this. He had been a victim due to all the trouble he'd gone through, but all he did was obey the count's orders, so the majority of the profits should be going to the old couple who owned the main store, and to me.

I mean, really.

And I shouldn't have to trouble myself by going to see him. He should be coming to see me.

"I apologize for all the inconvenience..."

It wasn't really the realtor's fault, and I understood that it would have been hard to decline a count trying to get their way. And the count's offer wasn't bad by any means, so the realtor was only doing his job as the middleman by selling it for a price they'd agreed on.

I understood.

I understood, but...

"You could have backed me up a little..."

Yeah, I couldn't help but think that. He probably wasn't expecting me to accept those terms, but the count surely had another line at the ready, and would've pressured me more and more. It was that one trick, you know, where you offered ridiculous terms, then tricked the customer into thinking you were giving them a good deal by compromising with slightly less ridiculous terms.

Since I easily accepted his initial offer, which had obviously been intended to be turned down, we were able to sign a flimsy contract that was easy to poke holes in. His final version was likely going to be much more polished.

But hindsight was always 20/20. It would've been one thing if he'd made any effort to protect his client, but he brought the count right over without giving me any sort of warning or providing me with a chance for me to think up a plan. He could've offered to bring the count by at a later date, or sent someone to warn me, or any number of other things.

And so, I asked the apologetic-looking realtor about the count.

"What did Count Oram say to you?"

"He asked me to buy back this property," he said, answering my question without seeming particularly bothered by it. "At first, he asked for the same price he paid previously and offered an inconvenience fee for the original owners and me, but I couldn't tell them to buy it back when they've already begun preparations to move into the city, where their son and his family live. He did purchase it for a great deal of money… Therefore, I told the count as such and we decided to purchase it ourselves. In other words, rather than acting as an intermediary for this property, we are now the owners."

Huh, he seemed awfully happy about that…

"So, how much did you lowball him for?"

"Huh…?" The realtor seemed surprised.

Don't play dumb!

That count was after the products being sold at Layette's Atelier and wasn't trying to make a quick buck. Sure, there were some poor counts, but this one seemed wealthy, and even had some guards with him. He knew when to back out, too, so he probably wasn't desperate for money. Most of all, he seemed worried about damaging his reputation from rumors about this incident going around.

…So, he wasn't stingy about paying the big bucks. I figured the only reason the realtor seemed to be in such a good mood was because he had made a profit from all this.

"…My rent is going down, right?"

"What?"

"My rent. It's going down, right?!"

"Huh? Well, uh…"

"My! Rent! It's! Going! Down! Right?!"

"…Y-Yes."

All right, victory!

And so, I confirmed that the ownership of the main store had been transferred to the realtor. We agreed that the contract for the branch store would be terminated today and that I wouldn't owe any rent for it. I mean, we'd already agreed to the rent being free for the first week.

After the realtor left and closing time came around, I locked the doors and closed the curtains. Then I put the entire shelf of products into my Item Box. The chairs, desks, and everything went right in there. I had intended for it to be a temporary branch in the first place, so I hadn't brought too much stuff. I still anticipated it taking three to four days, or possibly even longer, but it ended faster than I'd ever imagined.

Finally, I put a notice on the door:

"The branch store is now closed. We will resume medicine at the main store."

It was only for a day, but a few customers had gone to the main store and then came here after hearing we'd moved. We told them this was only temporary and that we'd return, but I figured a notice would still be necessary.

I returned to the main store empty-handed, escorted by Emile, Francette, and Roland. I would likely never return to this branch—no, the former branch store. Unless some weird noble showed up again, or something.

"I'm back!"

It was past closing time for the branch store, which obviously meant the main store was closed too. The door and windows were shut, but left unlocked. There was no way Belle would lock the door before I returned. Inside, Belle was waiting for my return at the register…

Or not.

Huh?

"Ah, Lad—I mean, Kaoru! You're late! Please, come help!"

Belle emerged from the back after hearing my voice. She was wearing an apron for some reason. She must've been pretty flustered, because she almost called me Lady Kaoru instead of just Kaoru, as she'd begun calling me lately.

"Huh? What? Why are you in such a rush?"

I stood there, confused, and Belle yelled, "The meals! We need to start preparations for tomorrow's box lunches! We won't make it in time if we start in the morning!"

I mean, we'd done prep work like soaking the ingredients last night for the meals we made today, but…

"Oh, that whole situation with the count is already taken care of. I returned the branch store and we'll be back to business here, as usual, starting tomorrow, so we don't need to do that anymore."

I thought Belle would be relieved, but she shook her head.

"No, that's not acceptable. Some of our customers who came in today returned in the evening. They put in orders for tomorrow's meals already… Their colleagues who came with them put in orders as well. The orders total up to over fifty meals! We can't simply make just those orders, so we'll need at least eighty…"

"Whaaat?!"

We'd made thirty meals to sell just for today. That was already hard enough with the prep work the previous night and waking up early to make them. And now we needed to make eighty?

"H-How many did we sell today…?"

"We're sold out, of course. It was a bit slow to begin with, without any advertising, but they were gone shortly after as soon as word about our box lunches spread. At this rate, we can sell out even if we make a hundred…"

"Wh-Wh-Wha?!"

Food service was hard work. Purchasing, prep work, cooking, customer service… The working hours alone were simply too long, with little downtime and tons of kitchen work. Miscalculate the estimated sales, and you'd end up with a mass of discarded food items. Though in my case, there wasn't much loss there, thanks to the Item Box.

In any case, I hadn't had any intention of staying in the food service industry!

"Then why did you start a box lunch shop?" Roland asked after hearing me mutter to myself.

"I wanted to sell something other than medicine and pottery or anything that seemed obviously profitable or desirable to nobles. But I also wanted to sell something that would make customers happy. The only thing I was confident in and could make normally was food… I thought it'd only be for a few days, and thirty a day wouldn't be a big deal… So, why'd you have to go and accept orders for tomorrow?!"

Belle made an apologetic face, but I was being unfair. This morning, we had no idea this would all be resolved in a day, and of course Belle would gladly accept orders if it made the customers happy. She did it for me.

It was true that I'd much rather sell out than have leftovers. Not because of the profit, but because the hard work we put into making those meals would make the customers happy. Belle must've felt the same way, since we'd made the meals together.

"…Sorry." I apologized sincerely.

"So, what should we do…"

I grabbed Francette by the shoulder as she tried to sneak out of there.

"You're not going anywhere." The more people, the better.

The guys? Nah, I doubted many people would want meals made by them. I doubted Emile and Roland would be of any use here, anyway.

"All right, let's do this!"

With that, I dragged Francette behind me as I headed toward the kitchen in the back of the store.

Oh, but first, I should get the medicine shelves out of the Item Box… I'll make the guys tidy up the shelves.

Chapter 25: What a Drag...

The morning of the fifth day since we began making a hundred packed meals per day…

We quickly made the things we couldn't prepare the night before, like food that went bad or lost flavor quickly, and completed the meals. There were a hundred in total: fifty pre-ordered meals, and fifty for general sales. We'd only taken up to fifty orders beforehand. This was the limit of how much we could make; or, to be honest, it was already past that limit.

It would've been easy to make them with my ability, but that wouldn't feel right. I didn't mind making medicine with it, but these meals were a different story. I wouldn't know the answer if you asked me what the difference was, but I, Kaoru Nagase, would not concede that point.

I felt like I had to protect that line, or I was afraid I'd make a barrel-shaped container full of gold and a little bit of medicine, or make a handsome man-shaped container with some medicine in his mouth, or other godless acts (and by "god" I don't mean that so-called god, but a real god like one they worship on Earth).

Speaking of those box lunches, we didn't just make the same one a hundred times; there were variations. It'd be too much trouble to make a big variety of meals, but we did make slight modifications on the side dishes depending on the preferences of whoever made them.

There were ten types of side dishes, and we each picked five of them as we put the lunches together. Not only were they made by Belle, Francette, and me, but Layette made some, too. While she didn't participate in the actual cooking, she picked out the side dishes and put them into the containers.

We stopped general sales once the number of pre-ordered meals pending pick-up and the number of meals in stock matched, so the pre-order customers who came after had to pick from whatever was left over. If they wanted a specific one, they'd have to come early. Everyone always picked the one with the shiitake-looking mushrooms simmered in sugar and salt, though. That really was a great dish, if I said so myself!

Oh, the condiments like soy sauce and sugar were made with my potion creation ability. That was still within the range of acceptability. I had to allow myself that, or it'd be too much. There had to be a line somewhere.

We put the boxed lunches out in the shop and had breakfast with the leftover dishes. Francette had woken up earlier to help out, but Roland was still sleeping at the inn. Emile was asleep upstairs, too. This meal was just for the girls who had helped make the lunches.

I was going to let Layette stay in bed, but she noticed me waking up in the morning and stayed awake ever since. It's said sleep brings up a child well, so I didn't want to wake her... But if I got a separate bed, she'd probably get upset.

Hmm...

In any case, the hunters and on-site workers who left first thing in the morning were already here buying box lunches, but... why did the Kaoru Box I made have the most leftovers?! Francette's"Fran Box, Belle's Belle Box, and Layette's Lay-unch Box all sold better than mine! Why?! I was confident mine had superior volume and balance for each dish! Besides, I was the one who thought up all the dishes and seasonings. This was unacceptable! I decided to ask the customers directly.

"Oh, the Fran Boxes are filling because it's like whoever made them forcibly stuffed the dishes into the box. It's just the right amount for us."

"The Belle Boxes don't have any fried foods or anything like that, so they're the healthy option. I cook the horned rabbits I catch on-site and the organs of bigger prey I can't take home, so this is just the right size."

"The Lay-unch Boxes are adorable. It feels like my daughter tried her best to make it for me."

"But you don't even have a daughter, wife, or lover…"

"Shut up! That's why I like them!"

"…Sorry."

Huh?

"E-Excuse me, umm… What about the Kaoru Box?"

"Oh, the Kaoru Box? Well, about that… If I had to describe it in one word, it's…"

"Yes…?"

"Average?"

I was dumbfounded. Speechless.

"Oh, I mean, it's good, though. The Kaoru Box tastes good, too, of course!"

The customer quickly tried to make me feel better after seeing my dejected expression.

Of course it's good! They're all good, I'm the one who made all the dishes!

Urrrg... Damn it, I wasn't about to go down without a fight!

But everyone else's box lunches were specialized for a certain demographic, while mine was for the general crowd. Since I was so used to cooking for my family, I had a tendency to lean toward the average of what most people enjoyed. If I geared my box lunch toward a certain demographic, there might be customers who wouldn't have anything to buy because they didn't like meals that were too peculiar.

Box lunches have so much depth to them!

There had to be a good solution. Some way that would make all the customers happy...

Wait, why am I getting so worked up over this?! This whole pre-packed lunch thing was a tool for my plan, and I was only going along with it because it was too awkward to quit. It was a nuisance, and it took up so much of my time...

But seeing the customers deciding between the options with a serious face, then putting the boxes into their bags with a smile and looking forward to eating what was inside... It just gave me this feeling I never got when selling medicine or when I was an office lady in my previous life. It was... fun? Happiness? Something like that...

Argh, damn, I wish I could think of a good idea...

There were some customers who weren't out on day trips too. Maybe they needed something that would last? Maybe they also needed drinks?

Ahh, what's gotten into me...?

* *

"Battalion commander, the medicine shop sisters are here!"

"Let them through!"

The soldier who led us there announced our arrival as he knocked on the battalion commander's door, and we heard the lieutenant colonel's voice respond. The soldier then opened the door and let us into the room.

"Huh…?"

I was expecting the lieutenant colonel to be alone, since he let us in, but there were five men sitting around the table on guest sofas. Of course, one of those men was the lieutenant colonel. Judging by the number of lines and shapes of what seemed to be their rank insignia, the other four seemed to be of slightly lower rank than him.

"Ah, allow me to introduce these men. They are my subordinates, the commanders of the four companies. These two are the medicine shop sisters I mentioned before. She's the one who has been supplying us with the medicine you've all been fighting over."

"Oho, so this is her…"

"She's younger than I imagined. Quite impressive, claiming exclusive distributorship at her age…"

Maybe it was the lieutenant colonel's influence, or maybe they were all good people to begin with, but none of them showed me hostility or mocked me, and all seemed to be friendly. Though I supposed most people in positions of power wouldn't try to intimidate a commoner girl who was about the age of their grandchildren. An idiot wouldn't be able to climb to the rank of company commander. But, then, I suspected they had a different face for their subordinates and enemies.

"And I hear you handled a noble who tried to interfere in your business?" the lieutenant colonel asked.

News sure was quick to reach his ears. Or could it be, did he have me under surveillance...?

"...Well, I guess it was like swatting away an annoying bug."

"Hahaha, she's got some spunk!" One of the company commanders laughed out loud, rather than the lieutenant colonel. Rank-wise... he seemed like a captain or major?

In any case, the strap of the bag was digging painfully into my shoulder. I couldn't place it on the table in front of the sofas they were sitting on, what with all the paperwork on top of it, so I placed my bag on top of the lieutenant colonel's desk. Then I pulled out the boxes of medicine and lined them up. I'd thought about lowering the quantity for this delivery, but I reconsidered and brought the same amount as last time.

"So, the guard regiment and royal sentries haven't been getting any of the medicine..." I commented with a bit of an attitude, and the lieutenant colonel replied with a truly confused look on his face.

"What? What does this have to do with them? What are you talking about?" The look on his face told me he was genuinely confused by my comment.

So, it really wasn't out of any malice...

They were completely different organizations, so the thought had simply never crossed his mind. That was all there was to it. It wasn't that the lieutenant colonel was doing something bad on purpose. This was all caused by my lack of knowledge... It was my fault.

Just then, some document on the table entered my field of view.

"...Huh?"

There, it read:

"High grade soldier's disease medicine, 2 small gold coins. 10g pepper, 3 small gold coins."

It was cheaper than the selling and market price? The medicine was two thirds the price I was selling for. The pepper was probably about the same rate, considering the market price. I'd heard medical expenses were free for the army because they were covered by the kingdom. So what was with these prices?

"You're reselling them?! And in plain sight, without even trying to hide it! Are you friggin' kidding me?!"

Seeing the menacing look on my face, the lieutenant colonel and company commanders all stared with a blank expression. Even if the lieutenant colonel was the buyer, the expenses would be paid by the kingdom, and I'd been prioritizing their deliveries because he claimed it was for his soldiers. This was an absolutely immoral resale, and an act of embezzlement. I thought they would've learned from the incident with the noble that I wasn't the type to take this sort of thing lying down.

I put the medicine I'd laid out on the lieutenant colonel's desk back into my bag and hoisted it onto my shoulder.

"This will be the end of our little arrangement..."

"...Wait! Wait, wait, wait! What in the world are you saying? What made you so upset all of a sudden?"

The lieutenant colonel got up in a flush, without even trying to cover the documents on the table. Such nonsense...

"Just what is this document?! High-grade disease medicine for two small gold coins, 10 grams of pepper for three small gold coins?! Your medical expenses are free, aren't they? What are these prices, then?!"

"Huh...?"

After my angry outburst, the lieutenant colonel's blank expression turned to that of shock. "Y-You can read this?!"

He must have assumed I could speak, but not read or write. Who did he think wrote the letter I gave to the child from the orphanage last time?

"I know how to read and write the language of this kingdom!"

"N-No, I understand that. I'm asking if you're able to read this coded message. We confiscated it in a place we suspect is the contact point for the group reselling military property on the black market."

"...Huh?"

"..."

"...Whaaat?"

"..."

"Whaaaaaat?!"

"The ability to communicate, read, and write in any language here."

Coded messages count as a "language" too?

"G..."

"'Guh'...?"

"Gyaaaaaa!!!"

I slowly put my bag back down on the lieutenant colonel's desk, then took out the medicine boxes and laid them out next to the bag.

"L-Let's pretend that didn't happen..."

"Now, wait just a minute!"

...Yeah, didn't think so.

I was then questioned rather fiercely.

"Explain yourself! How are you able to read the resellers' coded message?! No, I don't suspect you, so you don't need to look so scared. It wouldn't make sense for you to read it aloud if you were one of them. Unless you were incredibly stupid, that is. And I know you are not… Well, you're not that stupid."

"Why did you just rephrase that?!"

Damn it. I couldn't really deny that. It may have been Celes's fault, but it was true. I had messed up big time here.

I have to find an excuse!

"I-It's because this is a really easy code, one that can't even fool a child. Anyone could decode it at a glance!"

"…A team of military specialists has been working on it for three weeks now."

An awkward silence filled the room.

I have to get through this somehow!

It seemed like a series of meaningful letters when I first saw it without thinking, but looking at it carefully, I could see the structure of the sentences. Of course, my ability to "read and write" meant that I'd be able to write as well as I could read it. To write it, I'd need to be able to understand the rules of how the text strings were laid out.

"Um, first we read the text vertically… and the first number that appears is four, right? So you convert all the characters to the one four spots before them. And the second number going down vertically is three, so we skip three spots each and pick up the character there, then line them up. Then…"

The men jotted down notes in a hurry as I explained. Once my explanations were complete, the lieutenant colonel posed a question.

"…So you did this extremely complicated conversion process in an instant? All in your head, without taking any notes?"

I'd expected him to point that out, but I was prepared with an answer.

"Huh? Is there a need to take notes on something this easy?"

Aaaaaagh! Such a cringey line!

But I had no other way to explain it, so I had no choice!

"..."

...I want to go home.

"How would you like to join the military? If you join now, I'll let you become an intelligence officer as a major—no, a first lieutenant."

Oooh, a first lieutenant! A military officer and a leader! That was some favorable treatment, skipping right to a leadership position! Maybe he was offering a rank as a military officer instead of a civilian employee to make it harder for me to quit?

"Like hell I'm joining!"

Haah... haah...

I declined their attempts to get me to stay, and managed to get back home. Layette had blended in with the background and was apparently bored the whole time, unable to understand the conversation.

Um, sorry about that...

When we got back to the shop, Belle and Emile passed over the shopkeeping duties to us and departed to do some hunter work. They were off to hunt some beast instead of harvesting today. It was good to see that they were progressing.

Layette sat on my lap and helped me keep shop, as usual. The box lunches had been sold out for a while now. I sold some medicine for stomachaches and soldier's disease to the customers who came in occasionally.

Soldier's disease affected the average civilian, too, of course, but it wasn't nearly as prevalent as it was in the military, so there wasn't too big of a demand for it among civilians. Not many people spent their time sweating all day or walking around with leather shoes that didn't breathe well, after all. Besides, closed-toe leather shoes were expensive. Even soldiers would have had a hard time affording them if they weren't supplied by the military.

I made the stomach pain medicine in such a way that it killed off parasites, killed bacteria from food poisoning, broke down toxins, and relieved pain from internal diseases, curing them slightly, all in one dose. There'd be trouble if rumor spread that my medicines could cure any common illness, so I had to control myself.

Then, once the customers had stopped coming in…

"Excuse me, may I purchase five bottles each of the shampoo, cosmetics, and the perfumes you provided as samples the other day?" a maid asked as she walked up to the counter. I didn't recognize her face, but knew what she was talking about right away. She was a servant for the wife of the noble who had tried to monopolize the soldier's disease medicine, and I didn't even know her name.

Five sets of the shampoo and cosmetics would be thirty small gold coins. I could probably upcharge the perfumes to three small gold coins, so five bottles for fifteen.

Let's go with forty-five small gold coins total!

"I'm sorry, but the perfume is a bit pricey, so the total will come to forty-five small gold coins. Is that okay?" I asked hesitantly, but the maid was unfazed.

"Yes, my mistress has provided me with ten gold coins…"

Noooooo! I should have upcharged even more! She must've thought I undercharged last time and lost money just to appease her, or assumed the perfume was ridiculously expensive because it was only offered as a sample without being sold…

In any case, I blew it! It seemed like I could've asked for seventy small gold coins, which would've been seven gold coins…

No, no, hold on. If I charged that much, it would become the regular price, and the average citizen wouldn't be able to buy it! I didn't mind pricing the luxury items like cosmetics and perfume a little higher, but I had to keep the shampoo affordable.

As such, I reconsidered and began wrapping the products, and was in the process of doing so when a question came to mind.

"How is your mistress doing? Is her hair and skin looking well? Has she been talking about them to other noble ladies and gentlemen?"

It was market research for the advertising situation. We at Layette's Atelier use the latest business strategies as the leading enterprise in the industry!

"Oh, yes, she certainly has... Her hair is silky, her skin is smooth and supple... She's been saying rather excitedly that it's as if she's back in her younger years..."

Huh? I mean, they were definitely more effective than the ones on Earth, but their effects shouldn't have been that drastic... Oh, maybe because the effects of the shampoo and conditioner were so clear to see, so she thought they were more effective than they actually were? Like that placebo effect thing. Maybe, next time I see her, she'll thank me in Russian.

...Wait, no, that's "spasiba!"

"So, did she mention it to her other noble friends?"

"Oh, absolutely! Everyone has been envious and asking what her secret is, to which she responds by smiling and laughing. She looked ever so evil... I mean, happy."

Ah, that was goo— Wait, what?

"They ask her what her secret is...? Wait, what about advertising our shop? She hasn't mentioned where she got them...?"

"Huh? What are you saying? Do you think a noble mistress would willingly give up a secret that gives her an advantage in beauty? Is your head okay?"

Gahhh! No wonder there hadn't been any beneficial effects from the advertisement… I was expecting her to spread word about my cosmetic products, so I hadn't been advertising those at all! I didn't want too many customers coming in and going overboard. But now…

That's it, I'll show her!

"…Please, come here."

"Huh? Wh-What are you…"

I grabbed the maid by the arm and took her into the back room. I pointed with my chin, and Layette quickly entered to switch the sign at the door to indicate we were on a temporary break.

"Wh-What, what are you… Aaahhh!"

One hour later…

A maid with soft, flowy hair, glowing skin, and perfect makeup staggered out of Layette's Atelier, smelling wonderful. Her steps seemed a bit unsteady, but she looked happy as she took the shopping bags home.

"All right, advertising pillar number two has been erected! A commoner will have no choice but to answer if a noble or person in power questions her! Muahahaha!"

But even after that, the cosmetic products didn't sell much. This was the obvious result.

As soon as the mistress received the products, she told her maid to keep her mouth shut. She then prevented her from appearing before guests until her makeup and the effects of her hair treatment were completely gone. On top of that, the mistress examined the makeup put on the maid and practiced on her servants to recreate the effect, improving her techniques even further…

Chapter 26: Treasure Hunt

"Is the owner here?!"

After the rush for the box lunch had passed, a single soldier made his appearance. He was about forty or so, and seemed to be somewhat important. Well, in terms of rank, not his attitude.

"Ah, you're here! There's something I want to ask of you!"

He seemed familiar… Oh, he was one of the four company commanders at the lieutenant colonel's place!

"U-Umm, how can I help you…?" I couldn't just agree to help without knowing what he wanted.

"Yes, about that…" The commander lowered his voice and looked around cautiously. "It's actually a private request. Could I ask you to join me at my residence?"

"Huh…?"

I wasn't sure what to do. Considering his position, I didn't suspect that he was planning to do anything funny to me. Though, there were two possible exceptions.

One, this man was actually a member of the group responsible for illicitly selling military goods on the black market, and came to eliminate me because I could decode their messages. They could change the code, but I might end up decoding it again, so he may be coming to get rid of the issue at the source.

Two, he was a pedo and had the hots for me.

No no no. No way!

If he was here to kill me, he wouldn't have come here in person so early in the morning. He would have one of his men take care of it at night.

Besides, an older, strait-laced looking man like him couldn't be a pedo… Well, he could, but I didn't think he was the type to try and bring me to his place uninvited.

Plus, this seemed sorta fun. I'd been getting dragged into trouble and running around being busy as of late, so I wanted a little change of pace.

It also wasn't like I was hurting for money. Yes, I was running a business, so I would do my best to maximize profits. If I sold at prices so low that it disrupted the market, or ran my business without putting any thought into it, I'd be causing trouble for the other merchants and insulting the god of trade. That sort of thing was unforgivable to me.

So…

"The excursion fee will be one small gold coin."

"Y-Yes, of course… Thank you!"

Of course I'm going to charge him.

"Let's go out, Layette."

"Okay!" Layette responded cheerfully and began shutting the wooden windows. The windows and back door upstairs were already closed, so we just needed to lock the entrance and we were good to go.

"My residence is about twenty minutes from here."

Ah, the other side of the royal palace. It was a bit far… though I guess it really wasn't, by this world's standards.

Belle and Emile had left for their hunter jobs a little earlier, so I closed the shop temporarily. We began moving on foot, with Layette tagging along.

The company commander seemed to be a noble, but he was also a military officer, which might explain why he had walked to my shop instead of riding a carriage. We didn't bother preparing one or looking for a public cab.

I, too, had to exercise once in a while or I'd get out of shape, and not exercising wouldn't be good for Layette's growth either.

I glanced behind us on the way, and noticed Francette and Roland were following. Were those two always staked out at the shop? From where? When, and how long? Did they ever rest? I needed to ask them sometime. They weren't just standing out in the alley all day every day, were they?

What kind of exploitative business am I running?!

And so, we arrived at the company commander's house.

Hmm, judging by the building construction and distance from the center of the royal capital, his social standing wasn't too high. Maybe he was the equivalent of a baron or viscount? The lieutenant colonel and battalion commander was a count… or rather, he was the third son of a count, and probably wasn't going to inherit the title, so I supposed the lieutenant colonel wasn't too high in standing, either. It simply meant the other nobles would be polite toward him because of his family's authority.

We passed through the gates and headed toward the entrance, when…

"Welcome home, Master."

Whaaat?!

He was the head of a noble house?! Wouldn't that mean he was higher in the noble hierarchy than the lieutenant colonel? While he was just from a count's family, even if the company commander was just a baron or viscount, comparing an untitled third son and the head of such a household...

But getting on the bad side of such a household would be social suicide... I suppose these power dynamics are pretty complicated.

Even so, they were superior and subordinate in the same military, so it didn't really matter. Whether the military or a company, rank and position within that organization was everything. Their families, parents, ages, and academic backgrounds had nothing to do with it.

So how dare that shitty, ordinary employee give his mild-mannered chief clerk attitude... No, no, that was all in the past now. Moving on...

Oh, I should confirm now, so as to avoid any accidental discourtesy later.

"E-Excuse me, Mr. Company Commander, are you the head of your house?"

"Hm? Oh, I suppose I haven't mentioned it yet. Yes, I am Seyvos von Lasrich, Viscount Lasrich."

I knew it!

I didn't find any noble intimidating at this point, though. I was a woman who yelled at royalty, after all.

Muahaha...ha...

I wasn't gonna get punished for being improper some day, was I?

We were led to the company commander's... study? Office? That sort of room. He dismissed his family and servants, so it was just him, me, and Layette (in "fly on the wall" mode).

Now, for the main reason we were here…

"I've brought some tea for you."

Oh, tea and snacks? Don't mind if I do…

The maid left after placing the tea set and snacks, and we were finally about to move on to the main topic.

Munch, munch…

Yeah, there was Layette, munching away at the snacks…

I took a sip of tea. The company commander, seemingly out of habit, had walked at a marching pace as he led us there, so I was tired and thirsty from the trek. Sure, that was all fine and dandy for a military officer, but he could've been a bit more courteous to the ladies…

No, never mind! I'm sorry for acting self-important to an oh-so-mighty married person when I'm just a single woman who can't get a man!

I drank some more tea.

"So, about my request… I want you to find the location of some treasure for me."

Bwargfh!

I nearly spat out my tea, but just managed to stop myself. The company commander was wearing expensive-looking—well, certainly expensive clothes, and the sofa and carpet were similarly luxurious. I couldn't possibly spit here, so I desperately fought back the impulse and swallowed, nearly suffocating as a result.

"Why would you tell me this now?!"

Damn that open-mouthed, blank expression. He had no self-awareness! I'll make him spit out his drink in front of the lieutenant colonel some day!

In any case, an explanation. I needed him to explain himself before we could move on.

According to him, the house of Viscount Lasrich wasn't very wealthy. I mean, the head of the house was in the military… though, apparently, they weren't quite poor either. He joined the military because his older brother was supposed to have inherited the house and title, but had died suddenly. However, he wasn't allowed to leave the military for personal reasons, so he left the management of his territory to his younger brother and moved to the viscount's residence in the royal capital, managing his military duties and his house's social duties. This kind of story wasn't uncommon among the nobility.

So, what was the issue here?

…Money. They didn't have any.

So they are poor!

They'd used up all of their food in storage due to poor harvests for several years straight, so they had to stock up on food with the gold coins in their vault. Still, the surrounding territories were experiencing poor harvests too. Getting food delivered from far-off lands was pricey, and those shipments were prone to being raided by bandits and desperate peasants from other lands trying to feed their families. The costs piled up, as they needed to pay escorts to protect the goods. They somehow managed to gather the average annual yield of food this year, but their vault and stockpiles were nearly empty. If something else were to happen in this state…

Even if they had a decent harvest, something like an epidemic, a large-scale bandit raid, or any sort of other trouble could be that fatal straw that broke the camel's back.

Normally, this would've pretty much been checkmate. They'd have no choice but to take a loan from some big-time noble, basically becoming slaves and besmirching the name of his viscount house.

"Normally," of course.

The house of Viscount Lasrich actually had a hidden fortune. Or, more accurately, should've had one.

Several generations ago, a large, unmanned ship drifted up to Viscount Lasrich's seafront territory. No one recognized the ship, but its passengers had all perished and there was no food or water on board. However, the cargo and safe were left untouched. It was all non-edible items meant to be used for trade, such as ceramics, swords, and massive quantities of gold coins and jewelry. The viscount at the time was facing a similar danger as the current situation, secretly converted some that treasure to local currency, and used it to get through hard times. As for the remainder...

"Here it is. Please, decode it for me!"

With that, the company commander produced a sheet of parchment.

"This document has been passed down among the heads of the house throughout the generations. The location of the fortune was relayed via word of mouth, but the head of the house from three generations ago died in an accident before he was able to pass down that information... But now, my land needs it desperately! Please, read this document and find out where the fortune is!"

Ah, so that was why he asked for my help. In case the fortune's hiding spot didn't get passed down to the next generation, it was kept in writing with a coded message.

Yeah, it was important to keep backups.

But that stinkin' section chief didn't take backups for three whole months?! Who had to clean up after that whole... No, the past. Moving on...

He handed the parchment to me, and I began reading through it.

"Only when the province of Lasrich ever faces great danger, the resources have been exhausted, and there are no other possible courses of action, the fortune that has been passed down may be used. Corlacus von Lasrich."

That was all it said.

"How am I supposed to know thaaat?!"

Haah... haah... haah...

I threw the parchment down on the ground, breathing heavily, and the company commander stared at me, dumbfounded.

Oh no, I have to say something!

"How is this friggin' thing supposed to help me find it?!"

No, not like that!

"I-I don't understand how... Ugh, I'm creeping myself out!"

I put on my customer service smile as well as a feminine act, but it only made me writhe in embarrassment.

The company commander's eyes went wide with confusion.

"It's not even coded or anything! How do you expect me to find it with this?!"

"What? But I thought you could understand the writer's intent behind the text..."

He seemed genuinely surprised.

The heck is that?!

"I'm not some god! I can understand the content of the text because of my linguistic abilities, but that doesn't mean I can read the writer's residual thoughts! So, 'How's 'bouta cuppa joe?' might sound like, 'Would you like to have some coffee?' But it wouldn't sound like, 'Hurry up and go home, you're staying too long!'"

He didn't understand what a "cuppa joe" was, but seemed to have an idea of what I was trying to say.

"I... I see..." He slumped his shoulders.

I felt kinda bad for him...

Oh, fine. He did pay my service fee, after all...

"Umm, well, there's not much we can do about the message, but you just need to find out where the fortune is hidden, right?"

"Y-Yes, that's correct, but... Due to it being too risky to leave it in my lands near the border, and the fact that whenever the fortune was to be used, whether it be for food or political funds, the payment would be done in the royal capital... I'm certain it was placed here in the royal capital somewhere, but neither my father or grandfather ever found it, and I certainly haven't. I doubt it would be so easy..."

I brought the bag on my shoulder just in case of something like this. I stuck my hand inside the bag...

A healing potion inside a super high-performance, super portable metal detector-type container, come out!

...and I pulled out a shady-looking device.

"Huh? What is that...?"

"A metal detector. Basically, it's a device that detects nearby gold and shows you where it is."

"Whaaat?!"

The company commander raised his voice in surprise... Wait, no, this explanation could give him some unwanted ambitious ideas!

"Oh, it only reacts to refined gold with high purity, so it won't be any good for finding gold mines or anything like that. The detection range is very short, so its usefulness is limited, and it's also quite expensive, prone to breaking, and pricey to fix..."

I tried painting the metal detector as something that wasn't very useful, but he gave me a dubious look.

Oh well, time to get the request over with.

"So, you push this button and..."

I activated the device, and an arrow floating in a clear, glass sphere began spinning, then stopped, pointing in a certain direction.

"This way!"

I looked up cheerfully from the glass sphere… only to find that the pointer was pointing directly at the company commander's pocket.

"Ahhh…"

Yeah, that sure was the closest, refined piece of gold. As for my own money pouch, that was inside the Item Box, so it wasn't detectable by the device.

"O-One second please…"

I averted my eyes from his suspicious expression, then began operating the metal detector. It was an item I'd thought up, so it went without saying that its capabilities and controls would be as I imagined them to be. There was no way I wouldn't be able to use it.

"Let's see, I'll exclude your money pouch from the possible targets and set it to detect 300 grams of gold or more…"

A so-called fortune would surely be that much gold or more. There could also be some precious jewels or pearls or something, but there was probably some gold too. Maybe as ingots, or in coin form. What kinda fortune would it be without any gold? But if that were the case, it'd be time for the jewel detector device to shine.

Okay, let's try that again…

The needle pointed at the wall of the room, but we obviously went outside through the door instead of breaking the wall down. Of course, I'd go ahead and break into it if it pointed at the same wall from the other side.

When I entered the hallway, the needle didn't point at the neighboring room, but somewhere farther.

Good, good...

I kept following the pointer, and it took me to a certain room.

"This place is..."

The company commander had a pensive look on his face. He then seemed to make a decision, nodded, and produced something from his pocket. It wasn't a money pouch, but a bunch of keys. Maybe there weren't enough of them to call it a "bunch," but several keys were bundled together by a thin chain, which seemed to be connected to some inner part of his clothes.

He took one of the keys and unlocked the door to the room. Apparently, this room was important compared to the others.

He followed me inside, and...

"Whoa..."

It was a storeroom... no, more like a treasury or a vault room. In any case, it seemed to be where their wealth was stored. There were no windows, and until the company commander lit a lamp, the light coming in from the open door was the only source of illumination. And what was revealed by the lamp light was...

"...It's a storeroom?"

All sorts of junk... er, ornaments and mysterious objects were on display throughout the room.

Hold on, I shouldn't be calling it a storeroom. I was just thinking it was a "vault room"! Why did I have to be so blunt...

"Haha... I've already sold off anything that could be of any value. All that's left now are things that wouldn't fetch a good price, or objects that have great sentimental importance to the house of Lasrich. Despite the amount of objects in here, they're basically worthless in terms of market value. Though they're still treasures to our house nonetheless."

"…I'm sorry."

I was being too insensitive. All I could do was apologize.

Then, the direction the metal detector was pointing was…

"A big safe sitting next to the wall."

…Thanks, Captain Obvious.

"…"

The company commander was at a loss for words. The look on my face probably looked just like his.

There were gold coins inside the vault?

No duh, dingus!!!

"…"

"…"

"Well, we may as well open it…" he uttered after an excruciatingly long few seconds had passed. It seemed his hope was rapidly diminishing.

Hmm…

He brought out his keys again and opened the safe. Inside…

There were about twenty gold coins. In this world, that was equivalent to about 2,000,000 yen, so it was a decent amount of money. But even though it was a smaller viscount's house, it was extremely shabby for the contents of a noble house's safe.

"O-One second please!"

I messed with the settings on the metal detector again, excluding the safe from the potential targets. I checked the pointer again. It spun around…

Yup, nothing detected within range. Thank you very much!

The company commander seemed to understand the situation from the movement of the needle and the look on my face.

"Haha..."

"Ahaha..."

"Ahahahaha... Haah..."

Womp womp.

There was a dull look in both our eyes. Apparently, there was no mountain of gold ingots or coins in this residence...

Hey, wait a minute! What settings did I use when I detected the company commander's money pouch earlier? Right, I'd set it to detect "300 grams of gold or more"!

The gold coins here weighed less than ten grams each. They felt slightly heavier than a 500 yen coin, so I estimated they were about eight to nine grams. About the same as a quarter ounce gold coin from Earth? This meant that even if it weighed more from being mixed with other alloys to improve its hardness, twenty coins would only be about 150 grams of gold or so. Wouldn't the detector not react to that then?

I messed with the metal detector in a hurry, then removed the exclusion for the safe. Then I set it to detect 500 grams or more.

...The needle pointed at the safe. I leapt out of the room, and the company commander followed me hurriedly, wondering what was going on. Where I was going, of course, was the room on the other side of the wall where the safe was stored. That room was unlocked, and it seemed to be a sort of office for the company commander, or rather, the viscount. Though I supposed no one would put a nursery next to a vault room, all things considered.

It crossed my mind that maybe I was being incredibly rude and improper. But oh well, I doubted the company commander was a stickler for such things.

And so, I looked at the needle inside that room.

...Yeah, it was pointing toward the direction of the neighboring room, where the vault room was.

"Let's tear down this wall!"

"R… Right!"

The servants were called, and we began carefully tearing down the wall. We didn't do it from the side where the safe was because it would've been too much trouble to move the safe out of the way.

As the wall was peeled off, we finally hit metal! Yup, it was the back of the safe sitting against the wall. Of course…

We seemed to penetrate all the way through. Inside the wall, there was nothing but the structures holding up the wall originally.

"…Well, that's about it for one small gold coin's worth…"

"Hold on! Wait just a minuuute!!!"

I tried walking away quietly, but the company commander grabbed me by the collar.

You'll go bald if you get so worked up, ya know.

But more importantly…

"My neck! You're choking my neeeck!"

Well, I should've seen that coming.

*　　*

"What is the meaning of this…?"

He was understandably quite upset. The servants had already been dismissed. I guess I can't blame him, considering I had gotten his hopes up, destroyed the walls of his residence, and ended up with nothing.

I had no choice, it was time to pull out my trump card!

"Jewel detectooor!"

I reached into the bag on my shoulder and pulled out a new device. It was a jewel detector-type potion container.

"Detection targets: Corundum, diamonds, pearls. Search radius: Eighty meters. Set! Ready!"

By setting it to search for corundum, which included rubies and sapphires, as well as diamonds and pearls, it would definitely pick up any sort of treasure besides gold. And this time, I went with a PPI (Plan Position Indicator) scope to make it easier to tell where it all may be. It was that kind used on modern Earth that had a rotating radar antenna and blinked when it detected the target.

Yes, I was a woman who learned from her mistakes.

All right, begin detection! Switch on!

[No detection]

...Yeah, I figured as much. It was unlikely that something referred to as a "fortune" without specifying any precious jewel wouldn't contain any gold in the first place. But what was the deal here?

1. It was enshrouded in an anti-detection field.
2. The fortune was neither gold nor precious jewels.
3. It wasn't here.
4. It wasn't anywhere.
5. It was all in the company commander's head.

As well...

A. It never existed.

B. His ancestor had made up the story to give him hope.

C. It existed before, but had been all used up.

There were multiple possible answers.

I told the company commander as such, and he sandwiched my head between his fists and drilled my head with them. It was the so-called "umeboshi punishment." It was actually pretty effective.

Not to mention, the complete lack of emotion on his face made it scary. Really, really scary…

This was bad. I had to do something.

The company commander seemed to be getting anxious, and I felt danger looming in. I didn't want to be found floating in the river the next morning! I had to think! Think!

Ergh, grrr, hnnng!

Ah.

Aaahhh!

I took out the first detector that responded to gold again.

Switch on!

I pointed it in the direction it guided me, and it led me past the wall with the hole in it, then directly to the back of the safe…

I left the room wordlessly. The company commander followed me in a hurry.

I checked the direction in the hallway. Passing the vault room, I checked the direction again.

…Yup, that confirmed it!

I walked back into the vault room, which was left unlocked. It was left open! How careless! Though I guessed no one would just waltz into a noble's house in the middle of the day to steal something. Besides, a noble's house was never going to be completely empty. There'd always be several servants there at any given time.

The company commander and I stood before the safe. He had no idea what was going on, but seemed to know something was up from observing me. Then…

"I need something hard that you wouldn't mind getting damaged!"

"R-Right!"

He immediately produced a silver coin from his pouch. Well, it wasn't pure silver, so it was probably harder than "that."

So I took the coin and began scratching away... at the black-coated safe.

Scratch.

Scratch scratch scratch.

Scratch scratch scratch scratch scratch scratch...

The layers and layers of paint peeled away, revealing the safe's original surface below. A nice, golden color...

"Ah! Aaahhh!!!"

The company commander's eyes widened and he knelt to the ground.

"Ahhh... Father, my ancestor, and Goddess! The people of Lasrich will overcome this crisis and gallantly strive toward the future..."

"...But considering you keep facing danger with bad harvests and such, you'll eventually use this up and die out..."

"Q-Quiet!"

He was actually pretty mad, maybe because I'd ruined his heartfelt moment.

"How much of this fortune do you plan on using?"

"Huh? Oh, I don't plan to use any."

"Wha...?"

He explained that they had managed to power through this bad harvest by using their food storage and some of their viscount household's funds, along with a small loan.

"Word of my house's fortune became quite a big topic at the time. Thanks to the rumor that the House of Lasrich has a reserve for truly desperate times, it gives the impression that we're still not in enough trouble to withdraw from it, that we can fall back on it to repay any loans if necessary. This allows us to acquire loans with little to no collateral."

Huh, I knew there were many drawbacks to people knowing you had money, but this was a perk I hadn't thought of.

"But if something were to happen before we could build up our reserves again, one small incident could have bankrupted us. If that were to occur, we would've had to borrow money from a lord of a big territory and effectively become part of their territory, or we would have had to return the land to His Majesty to have it merged with another territory… In either case, we would have been treated differently compared to their original residents in matters such as taxes, and there would have been no benefit for my people. No matter what may happen to us, I have to avoid this at all costs… This was why I absolutely had to find that fortune now."

Wow! Such a good person!

Oh, but what if people find out that he found the fortune?

"Wouldn't it be an issue if the government finds out though? With taxes and demands for payment to the treasury and such…"

"No, there's no need to worry about that." He dismissed my concern right away. "When my ancestors first discovered the fortune, they notified the kingdom and paid taxes for it properly. That's why no one doubts the existence of it. No fool would lend large amounts of money without collateral based on hearsay alone. Besides, if everyone knows we have a fortune, there's no problem, since we do actually have one."

I-I see…

His ancestors must've been straitlaced and honest people. But this was the ancestor of a company commander who used his personal funds for the people of his fief, so it probably ran in the family. I personally didn't dislike people like him, so I decided to give him some advice. Some irresponsible advice that wouldn't be my problem if he actually followed it.

Hey, I wasn't the one who'd be paying for it.

I sound so evil right now...

"...Why don't you blow it all?"

"Huh?" He looked surprised.

"I mean, use up all that fortune your ancestors left for you!"

"Wh-Wh-Wha..."

What good were life and money if you couldn't enjoy them?

"You've had bad harvests a bunch of times before, which will surely occur again, right? How many times do you think you can endure that before your fortune dries up?"

"Ugh..."

From the sounds of it, it was used several times in the past already anyway.

"And if a bad harvest had such terrible repercussions, what if you have continuously devastating harvests? What if it goes on for years? Fluctuating weather like cold summers or pest issues could easily go on for years. In that case, the amount of food you'd need to buy from other regions would skyrocket. In fact, they may not sell you anything because they'd think of their own fief's people first."

"U-Uuugh..."

I must've scared him, because he was starting to look pale.

"Instead of patching the issue whenever something happens, you should stop the issue at its source. If you don't fix the fundamental problem, any money you throw at treating the symptoms will be wasted."

"H-Hmm... You say that, but what can I do? We're a poor region with little fertile land..."

Yeah, I knew that. If that hadn't been the case, he wouldn't have been in this situation so many times before, when the country as a whole wasn't having bad harvests. I couldn't say anything for sure without confirming the full situation, but I did at least have a starting point.

"Please consider the reason for the bad harvests not just in your region, but in other places with similar conditions, and compare them to the times where you didn't have such issues. If it was because of a cold summer, you could get seeds for crops that are strong against the cold from the northern regions. If it was because of droughts, you could dig a deep well or channel a waterway from a nearby river. You could also diversify to minimize risk by growing not just grains, but corn and potatoes as well... Potatoes can grow quickly even in sterile lands and they're full of vitamins. They're also resilient to the cold, droughts, and weather changes in general, so they're highly effective as a safety net. It may not be an attractive option for sales, but human lives come before profit, right?"

"Y-Yes..."

The company commander seemed a bit hesitant. He wasn't an idiot, so of course he knew about potatoes. But countries around here had it in their minds that potatoes and corn were feed for livestock. They'd eat anything if they were starving, of course, but they didn't really consider growing them for the purpose of human consumption. Grains and leafy vegetables were the core of the crops meant for human food, with wheat being mainly used for paying taxes. Peasants usually ate rye, oats, and barley, since they were so easily grown, even if the land wasn't in perfect shape or there wasn't enough water.

But with the level of civilization in this world, harvesting grains was highly inefficient. About 300 kilograms were harvested per acre, which wasn't too bad for being roughly equivalent to the Middle Ages of modern Earth, but it was nowhere near the three to four tons that could be harvested with modern agriculture. A good harvest here would be 500 to 600 kilograms. Also, in the case of potatoes, one acre could yield about 30 tons on modern Earth.

"I understand this is so much to take in so suddenly. Please just think about it."

No lord would just agree right away to a spontaneous suggestion from some random girl who didn't know about managing territory or agriculture. And if there was a lord like that, it'd probably be best to stay away from their lands. He might try to push the blame from his failures onto you…

I wasn't going to help him with any internal affairs cheats, though. That'd only be an extreme risk for me, with few possible benefits. We'd be talking about years of time, too. I'd offered some simple advice because I was already involved, but I wasn't going to take responsibility for any of it. I'd already provided one gold coin's worth of work.

"Well, then, I'll be excusing myself…"

Layette was getting bored with nothing to do. It seemed she didn't like staying at the noble's residence either. I had to head back to try and appease her. Lunch time was approaching, too.

And so, I tried to depart.

"Wait, I can't just let you leave after all you've done! We're preparing lunch, so please have some before you go."

"Okay!" Layette and I immediately replied in unison.

Joining a noble family's meal was a rare opportunity. Though, I guess we'd technically be joining nobles for a meal if I had made Roland or Francette pay for one, but that was different.

In Layette's case, this was a miracle that would've been impossible even if she was to be reborn ten times over. She might've been hesitant because she didn't know proper table manners or because she didn't want to impose, but for six-year-old Layette, this was a chance to eat delicious food, and that was all there was to it.

...Though, I didn't have much room to talk.

"You've been a great help today. I'd like to thank you on behalf of the house of Lasrich—no, for the entirety of the house of Lasrich's fiefdom."

The company commander formally thanked us before the tables full of food in the dining hall. Seated there were me, Layette, the company commander's wife, his two twenty-something daughters, and his sixteen- and eighteen-year-old sons.

This may have been a viscount's household, but they were still well-respected nobles, and they were a family all the more pleasing to look at too. Maybe they had inherited their ancestors' good-natured blood, because they all had gentle eyes. The company commander's sons seemed like they'd grow up to be dandy men when they were older, and I had high expectations for their futures.

...But why did they have such an all-star cast? And were those military outfits they were wearing? Their uniforms seemed much different...

I didn't even think it was a day off for them. Normally, this was the time people began eating and chatting, but the brothers looked at me with flushed cheeks and passionate eyes without touching their forks or knives.

...Had they fallen for me?

Maybe this wasn't a bad result. Becoming the wife in a small, somewhat poorer viscount's household, improving the agriculture and river management as we received the finances to do so, being taken care of by my mother- and father-in-law, having kids and living a fulfilling life with the population of the fief…

It seemed like it'd be a lifestyle of freedom, one where I didn't have to worry about getting by. There'd be no social hierarchy to concern myself with, and the company commander seemed like a good person who cared about his people.

Yeah, it wasn't a bad idea. If they ever tried to court me…

As I thought about it, one of the brothers approached me with a serious look on his face.

"Miss Kaoru, there's something I'd like to ask of you…"

H-Here we gooo!

"Wait, Big Brother, me first!"

Whoa! And sudden interference from his younger brother! Looks like I'm popular!

"No, I'm first!"

"No, me!"

Fueheheh, now was the time to bust out that line, the line I'd always wanted to say: "Please, don't fight over me!"

Ehe, fueheheh…

And finally, the two brothers turned toward me and shouted, "Please, give me some of your soldier's disease medicine!"

Of course.

…Yeah, I saw that coming.

Damn it! Got my hopes up for nothing!

…No, this was my fault for assuming, not theirs. To jump at the opportunity because of their looks and status without even confirming their personalities or anything… What was I, an unpopular thirty-something woman? Wait, my mental age, or the number of years I'd lived was over twenty-seven, so I pretty much was thirty!

Whoa, whoa, wait a sec. Since that asshole crown prince proposed to me, maybe I could relinquish the title of an unpopular woman?

No no no no, never mind! That didn't count!

"...Sure."

I stuck my hand in my bag, which I put next to the chair, then pulled out two bottles of the medicine that I'd created on the spot and slammed them on the table. I thought I'd concealed my displeasure, but I couldn't help the sullen look from showing on my face. The company commander looked a little anxious. He must've thought I was upset because they made such brazen requests at the dinner table or something.

...But suddenly, he started grinning at me.

Damn it, he figured me out!

Layette couldn't wait anymore and began chowing down. Actually, the dinner had already started some time ago, so there was no need for her to wait.

I began stuffing my face too, partly to hide my embarrassment.

...Mhm. As expected of a noble household's cooking, it was well-made with good ingredients and technique.

But...

"..."

The look on Layette's face screamed something was off. It was a look that said that the food wasn't much different from what we usually ate.

Indeed, I was pretty confident in the food I'd been making. Whenever I found good ingredients on the cheap, I stocked up on them and stored them in the Item Box. This ensured that I always had high-quality, fresh ingredients.

NOOO~!

......
GRIN

Then there were the plethora of seasonings I made with my potion creation ability. Not only that, but there had been times when I'd cooked instead of my mom ever since I was in middle school. This was how I'd mastered everything from prep work and cooking basics to complex cooking methods. So, because cooking in this world wasn't very refined, my cooking could hold its own against professional chefs!

Was it not fair that I used artificial seasonings? Yeah, I'd agree. In any case, the viscount's family seemed to think we were not-particularly-wealthy commoners and we'd been emotionally moved by such a lavish meal for the first time in our lives. A portly man, who I presumed to be the head chef, even came out from the kitchen, seemingly to get some satisfaction from seeing the reactions of us common girls, but had a disappointed look on his face upon seeing Layette's disapproval and me eating it normally.

Not my problem!

After the dispirited chef went back to the kitchen, we began having a pleasant chat along with the meal. Apparently, both sons were in the military, as I'd presumed, with one of them in the royal sentries and the other serving as a platoon leader in some other battalion. If he was a platoon leader, he was probably around the rank of a second or first lieutenant. On Earth, he probably would've graduated university, enlisted as a cadet, and have been at this rank a few years after graduating from the military academy...

Though in this world, the education they received from their tutors until they become adults at fifteen was considered the replacement for graduating from a university. This meant that, unless you were a noble or from a very wealthy home, you couldn't enlist as a cadet from the get-go.

Long ago, there were countries on Earth that had only allowed nobles to become officers, too. This country may have been considered progressive, considering there were officers who worked their way up from being common soldiers.

The sons had been sent to the sentries and a different battalion so they could avoid any aspersions cast on them from riding their father's coattails in the same unit. I was sure this wasn't a lie, exactly, but the true reason was probably the same one where a fisherman and his son didn't go out in the same ship. If there was ever a shipwreck, the family line would end right there.

But the royal sentries had more of an elite ring to it, so that could've been why the one son opted for it instead. It seemed like being in the sentries meant that he got to stay in the royal capital, too.

Hm... I'd only delivered the soldier's disease medicine to the sentries once before, and the other son was in a different battalion, which explained why they hadn't received any yet. Maybe they were even put at the back of the waiting list because people would assume they got it from their dad... But the company commander seemed like the type that would keep public and private affairs strictly separate.

Anyway, why were they home on a weekday, and in their military uniforms? And the daughters, judging by their age and clothing, seemed to be married already.

Oh, they must've taken some time off and gathered back home because they knew a few days ago that I'd be coming.

...Why, though?

I was sure the company commander had given me the original request because he was sincerely in trouble, but maybe he had a plan to get some sort of benefit from this visit if that ended up in failure? Maybe for some personal purpose related to the company commander, or rather, the house of Lasrich, that had nothing to do with the lieutenant colonel or the other three company commanders…

But even though he'd had his sons abandon their military obligations for the day and called his daughters over from their in-laws' homes, he probably had no intention of marrying his sons off to me. If that was the case, they would've explained as much, and the first words to me from their mouths wouldn't have been to ask for the medicine.

Damn it, is it because I look like a kid?!

No, no, wait a minute. Thinking about it, this was a country modeled with a class system in place. Even though a viscount was considered low-ranking among nobles, there was no way they'd marry off the first son and successor of the house, or the second son, who was next in line after him, to some (seemingly) underage girl of unknown origins who'd wandered in from another country. This even took into account whatever value I had to them. I mean, they could just get their family all chummy with me, make me one-sidedly fall for one of the sons, then take advantage of my usefulness by…

Hey, that's the exact situation I'm in now!

Damn it… Wait, stop that.

My word choice has been pretty unprofessional lately. These may just have been internal thoughts, but I was afraid I'd vocalize them some day if I kept thinking like this.

Calm down, me! Breathe in, breathe out… In… Out…

Oh, I know!

"Now that I'm of age, I'm hoping to find someone nice soon…"

I segued into one of the married daughters' in-laws' conversation by indicating my willingness to find a husband myself.

"Bffffff!!!"

...Why did they just spew out their drinks?! All of them at once, too!

"No, I mean, I'm an adult, and I run a medicine shop, and I'm Layette's guardian as well! I'm not a child who manages the shop or anything like that!"

Yes, I'd slowly spread word that I was of marrying age, so as to progress my search for a partner. I said I was of age instead of saying my actual age, because, well... I had no choice. I'd been treating the day of my reincarnation as my fifteenth birthday, which meant I'd be nineteen and a half now. There was no need to hasten my own deadline.

But I didn't want to lie and say I was fifteen or sixteen. Roland and Francette would only look at me weird if I did... Besides, if I returned to the kingdom of Balmore with my future husband, or if rumors about me reached that prince, the lie about my age would be exposed.

I couldn't get married by falsifying my age. I'd obscure it instead. No one would go out of their way to question a lady about her actual age.

"You have a child at your age?!!!"

"No! I'm just taking care of her! I'm not her actual mother!!!"

If that became a rumor, it'd be catastrophic in my search for a husband!

After all that, I explained how I'd saved Layette and became her guarantor and guardian, quickly dispelling that misconception. I was planning on taking care of Layette for however long I needed to, but it would negatively impact my search for a suitable marriage partner if people thought she was my daughter. Our relationship wasn't like that of a mother and daughter at all, anyway, so it'd be even worse for my search if people thought I was cold to my own daughter.

...Was having a child with me already a handicap? No, if a man didn't have the capacity to accept this, I wouldn't want to marry him in the first place.

I will find Layette a nice husband someday!

Just as I'd planned to for some time, I used my tear-jerker story of growing up poor and having little to eat to explain my small stature. In reality, my height was more than average for a Japanese person! Westerners were just too big!

On Earth, Westerners were also small when they were at this level of civilization, but that was due to their diet. They didn't have many opportunities to eat meat and lacked the nutrition to grow bigger. And if you were wondering why the people of this world were as big as people on modern Earth, well...

Even if they didn't go through the trouble of feeding livestock their low-yield crops, monsters would multiply on their own. Monsters, which needed to be hunted to secure the safety of the townspeople. Monsters, which had edible meat.

Yes, so long as you didn't care about taste or the toughness, monster meat was edible and cheap. Some of them were even pretty good, depending on the species. No one ate things like goblin meat, but orc and graybear meat were pretty good. Horned rabbits were easy to obtain,.too.

Nobles, who never ate monster meat, but only expensive deer and boars, would say, "I won't eat orc, only pork"... Probably not.

Also, boa juice made from boas. Was it made from boas or boars?! Well, it would have to be the snake kind, since it melted human bodies. Considering the rakugo story of "Jagansou"...

Long story short, the people of this world had the height and build of the Westerners of modern Earth, where meat consumption had increased.

Yup, really.

So, after talking for some time after, we were ready to go. They asked that I stay longer, but I couldn't just close down the shop for a whole day without any prior warning, especially when it wasn't even a holiday. We weren't just some general store, but a medicine shop where customers may very well urgently need our services.

"...I wonder what that dinner was for, anyway. Just for getting acquainted with his family?" I asked Layette, but she had no idea.

I thought about it some more as we walked, when suddenly...

"Layette?"

An older man who I didn't recognize called out to her. There was no way someone could recognize Layette out here when she hadn't ventured outside her rural village. If they did, then that would mean...

I was already protecting Layette's back as it crossed my mind. Roland and Francette appeared to cover my flank.

Where had they come from...?

Well, I guess this was to be expected. If not now, when were they going to spring into action?

The long, long, long, long, long, long, long time spent on standby was finally going to pay off. Of course they'd come flying.

Francette, can you stop grinning so happily like that? You're making it hard to tell who the bad guy is here...

Just as Francette bared her fangs...

"You're safe, Layette?! I'm so glad... Are these people your new masters?"

"Huh?"

Something was off here...

And so, the man told us his story.

A transaction akin to slave trading, where eighty years' worth of salary was paid upfront at an incredibly low rate for a merchant apprenticeship in another country. But these were measures taken in desperation, where the only options the peasants had were to either lower the number of mouths to feed or otherwise starve together as a family. The long contract term was to prevent the children from being taken away as collateral in case their family took on more debt. The price was cheap to make it easier for them to pay off the down payment through money they'd earned from tips and side jobs. They were effectively a regular servant who had their rent paid in advance, so they were able to live a normal commoner's life.

A live-in job that came with three meals a day... They could earn a bit of allowance on days off and go out freely. But what if they escaped? Someone would be sent to collect the down payment from their family, and it'd be impossible for a young child to survive in a foreign country where they didn't know anyone. The best they could hope for at that point would be to live in the slums and die early. Compared to that, a warm bed and three meals a day as a servant was far better.

It was, at the very least, the preferable option to staying home and having nothing to eat. They could even buy their own freedom with enough money saved, or even find someone to pay off the down payment, get married, and live a happy life. They'd be able to achieve happiness far beyond anything possible while starving back in their rural village.

"...Then, I regret to say, she was taken by a group of kidnappers. Even though I wouldn't be ashamed to do what we do in front of the Goddess, we could be accused of human trafficking according to the law. That was why I couldn't report the incident, and my only choice was to flee the city... I was afraid she was being used by a noble or some other wealthy person somewhere else by now. But to find that she's still safe and living a good life... nothing could make me happier."

There were tears in the middle-aged man's eyes as he spoke.

"Such a good person..."

If he was just a slave trader, he probably wouldn't have bothered to learn the faces and names of his "stock." Since he remembered Layette's name, it showed that he cared about her as a human being.

"So, what is Layette's living situation now? Did she get purchased or..."

"Y-You fool! What are you blabbering on about in a place like this?!" Francette yelled in a fluster.

Yes, slave trading was a serious crime. There may not have been much foot traffic past noon, but this wasn't something to talk about so blatantly out in the open.

"...Follow me!"

And so we moved over to Layette's Atelier. We kept the shop closed and everyone went upstairs.

"Layette is currently a normal person, an inhabitant of a fief, without being bound by contract to anyone. Here. This document proves it, signed by this territory's lord himself.

I pretended to reach into my pocket and pulled out various documents, and the man's eyes widened.

"These documents are official... So, this girl has achieved a normal, happy life..."

Yeah, but was he okay with that?

"But didn't you lose out substantially from this? You paid off Layette's parents, and they probably didn't get their money because the merchant never received her..."

He responded, "No, it's just business, so I'd already factored in some level of loss. It wasn't like I lost hundreds of gold coins from this incident. Besides, when I didn't report the kidnapping, I'd already abandoned my duties and rights."

It was the exact same textbook answer I'd heard from one of the lord's subordinates. I mean, I was glad he wasn't causing a fuss, but how was he such a good person? Just what type of merchant was he?!

"Um, you are a merchant, so maybe you shouldn't be so moral for the sake of your business..."

The merchant drooped his shoulders dejectedly at my advice. I guess he was already aware.

Francette's shoulders also drooped, seeing that her time to shine ended up being resolved just by talking. It seemed she had wanted to swing her sword and protect me from danger... But judging by the fact that our opponent was just a tired old man, that wasn't realistic in the first place.

In any case, it wasn't as if I was worried about it, but one of the pending concerns regarding Layette had been resolved. Now I had to look out for Layette's parents showing up and screaming to give her back, trying to sell her to the merchant again, giving her away to a neighboring village for ten bags of wheat, or making her work and take care of them, but I'd need to teach her so that wouldn't happen...

Hm, no, that wouldn't be necessary. Layette was six already, and very bright, too. She was smart enough to know what to do. Besides... as Layette watched the merchant go home with a cheerful expression, her hand was gripping mine tightly. She'd stay with me until the day she got married... I just had a feeling.

Oh, but I'd be getting married first, of course! I'd get married and take her with me.

...What if someone wanted to get married with both of us?

Obvious answer: He'd be judged by divine punishment!

Chapter 27: Complaint

"Is the manager here?" a portly, middle-aged man asked upon entering the shop.

If he'd been a normal customer, he'd have checked out the product shelves or asked if we had a specific item first. Therefore, this man was not a normal customer.

I smelled trouble. But he didn't seem like a noble, so I doubted it'd end up being too big of an issue. Maybe he had a question about a specific medicine, or some other business with me…

"Oh, yes, that would be me…"

"No, not the hired shopkeep. I want to speak with the proprietor."

Well, if he'd done even a little research, he would've heard about the child(ish-looking) manager here. Though I guess it was natural to assume I was hired as a salesperson and someone else was in charge of stocking medicine and paying the rent.

"…Yes, I am the manager and owner."

"What?!"

Yup, already used to that reaction…

"So you pay the rent here, stock the medicine, and sell it all?"

"Yes, I do. Can I help you?"

"…"

Huh, what's going on? He went quiet…

"Then tell me who your supplier is."

This again...

"Do you really expect a seller to blab about their supplier and products so easily? What, do you think I'm stupid just because I'm a girl? Are you a noble from somewhere?"

I was thoroughly annoyed at this by now, so I dropped the pretense.

"I-I am not a noble. I'm from the Association."

Huh? But there shouldn't be any organizations like a Merchants' Guild spanning across industry and commerce here...

Taxes were to be paid directly to the government. There were gatherings based on occupations, like the Blacksmiths' Association or Bread Baking Research Association, but membership for those groups was solely optional. Besides, in this town alone, there should've only been five other medicine shops besides Layette's Atelier.

"What is the association called? What type of organization is it? How big is it? And, uhh, how many members are in it?"

"Ugh..."

Why was he stammering now?!

"The Medicine Shoppe Association! Many of the medicine shops besides this one have joined already!"

"Huh...?"

So... three shops? If four had joined, he'd have said "all but one." If five had, he'd have said "all of them" had joined already.

"...I decline."

There was no reason to listen just because three shops went off and made a group. Not one bit. Their members could go ahead and follow whatever regulations they decided on. It had nothing to do with the rest of us, and they had no power to enforce anything.

"Why?! This is an official order from the..."

"Um, that doesn't mean anything to anyone who's not in your association. And what happened to the other two shops? Oh, if I join forces with the remaining two, we'd have an even power balance..."

"Wha..." The man became flustered.

Why was such a meaningless social gathering trying to enforce things for their selfish reasons, anyway?

"So, obviously, you're all going to tell me all of your suppliers, buying prices, compound ratios, and secrets, too, right?"

"What?! There's no way I could do that!"

He noticed Layette looking at him like a piece of garbage and cast his eyes downward, finally seeming to realize how ridiculous his demands were. The look of contempt coming from a pure young girl seemed to be pretty effective.

At least he was still familiar with the concept of "shame"...

"Why go through all this trouble...? We don't carry any medicine that would work on serious injuries or illnesses, and besides our featured soldier's disease medicine, we only sell things you could practically get anywhere else, like antidiarrhetics and antiseptics."

"But that soldier's disease medicine is a huge deal! People normally won't buy medicine unless they're injured or sick, but that can be sold indefinitely. And starting from the army, you can make connections with hunters, field workers, and some nobles, leading to the sale of other medicine. Not only that..."

Huh? But I wasn't making connections or upselling anything...

Oh, he meant that was what he would do.

"How can normal medicine be so effective?! Why should we get accusations of our products being fakes that deliberately don't cure people so we can make more money? Sure, we dilute it a little, but it's still somewhat effective if you drink enough of it!"

STAAARE

Ah…

I made my medicines to be effective, so of course they'd work. But I hadn't been making anything that could instantly fix serious injuries and illnesses like the Tears of the Goddess and other potions. The medicine's effects were meager, like curing stomach pain or preventing wounds from festering…

Wait, I guess it'd be pretty obvious with repeated use or when compared to medicine bought at other stores. It'd be clear to see the difference in efficacy and reliability…

Hold on, what did this guy just say?! He dilutes medicine that's already pretty weak…

Hmm, what to do…

I couldn't give him my supplier or manufacturing method, of course. Like, I literally couldn't. Neither of those existed.

Hmmmmmm…

I got it!

"Very well, I'll see what I can do. Please give me a few days."

"Ah, so you understand now! Then hurry up and make the preparations!"

"Yes, now, please give me the names of the shops who have joined the Medicine Shoppe Association…"

The man from the so-called Association gave me the names of the three shops and left with a spring in his step. He was probably full of hopes picturing massive profits rolling in in a few days.

"…Are you sure about this, Big Sis?"

Knowing my potions were created with my ability, Layette looked at me with concern, but yeah, there was no problem.

Come to think of it, Roland and Francette never showed up. It was just one merchant-looking guy, so maybe they thought he was a normal customer, or went off on a date together…

Nah. They wouldn't do that. I was positive they were watching me from somewhere.

...So creepy!

And so, I exited the shop and looked at the sign posted outside.

"Layette's Atelier"

Below it, "WE COMPOUND MEDICINE HERE" was written on a different plate.

Hmhm.

* *

A few days later...

"I-Is the owner here?!"

"Oh, you're the Medicine Shoppe Association guy from the other day..."

Yup, the guy barging in and screaming was none other than him.

"Wh-What is... Huh? Th-This is..."

Box lunches were on display in the shop, with even more variety than before. There was even a new system in place that allowed customers to choose their own side dishes. In addition, there were drinks and portable, nonperishable foods like jerky and hard bread, along with snacks, cookies, and such.

Everything besides the box meals was made to last a long time. It was too much of a hassle to cook them every day, and other than the box lunches, which would definitely be eaten that day, I was worried about the food going bad.

We'd purchased the ingredients from other stores and made them ourselves without using my abilities. We even offered a service where you could bring in your own containers to fill them up with drinks.

"Wha… Th-The medicine! Where is the medicine?!"

"Medicine? Please go outside and check the sign."

"What?"

The man stepped outside and looked up to find:

"Layette's Atelier"

"BOXED MEALS TO GO"

One big and one small sign had that text written on them. Next to the entrance was also a note:

"Due to complaints from the Medicine Shoppe Association (Cultivar Drug Store, Veilas Pharmacy, Mertolen Medicine Shop) claiming our medicine was causing trouble for their business by being too effective, we have stopped selling medicine at our store. We will continue doing business selling packed meals, and we hope for your continued patronage."

"Wha…" The man opened and closed his mouth repeatedly.

"We've stopped selling medicine to focus on box meals. Now your problem is solved!" I said as I smiled.

The man began screaming, red in the face, "This solves nothing! All three shops have been getting complaints non-stop, and all of our customers have moved to the two shops that haven't joined the association!"

Huh?

I wasn't necessarily hung up on running a medicine shop. I just wanted a place where I could interact with people while seeming like I was making just enough money to live a normal life without flaunting what I'd saved up. It just so happened that a medicine shop was the easiest way for me to do that, and while I didn't expect the box lunch shop to be a hit, it fulfilled that goal just as well.

I was getting a little annoyed by all the trouble brought in by the medicine shop, and selling box lunches was more fulfilling in the sense that I could see the customers' direct reactions. The prep work was hard, but at the end of the day, I felt like I did some good, honest work.

Even with the box lunch shop, I was making good use of the powers Celes gave me. I could make meals in bulk whenever I had the chance and store them in the Item Box, where they wouldn't degrade, so I wasn't so busy that I was always being chased by time. As the meals were sold, I could replenish them from the Item Box little by little, so there was little to no wasted food. The products were all hand-made by us, so there was a great sense of accomplishment and fulfillment that came with the work.

What a perfect job!

...But why was this old man annoying me with all his whining?

* *

"What's the meaning of this?!"

Oh, it's the lieutenant colonel.

"Meaning of what?"

"Don't feign ignorance with me! ...Though I suppose there would be no point in denying it. What is this? And what happened to the medicine?!"

Oooh, he seemed pretty mad.

"Oh, I closed down the medicine shop. The reason is just as it was written in the letter delivered by my messenger..."

"Stop fooling around! Then I just need to crush this so-called association? Should I crush the organization? Their shops? Or crush the owners themselves?!"

By "crush the owners," he probably meant physically...

But I had already sent away the association people the other day, so they no longer had anything to do with this.

My shop wasn't a medicine shop anymore.

"Well, this isn't a matter involving nobles or the military. It's just an issue between professionals in the same industry, so I don't think you should be stepping in. I don't think a military officer should intervene when it doesn't concern you..."

"It absolutely concerns me, you fool!!!"

Ahhh! He's actually really mad... Oh no!

I waved both my hands in front of me in a fluster.

Francette and Roland were glaring in our direction with their hands on the hilts of their swords, so I desperately tried to signal that everything was okay.

They looked like they were about to charge in with their swords drawn if I didn't call them off...

"What about our medicine?! Not just the soldier's disease medicine, but your medicine is known for being effective, so I had given orders to supply everything from your shop!"

Ahhh! That's why! That's the reason that suspicious "association" had suddenly appeared!

"Hm? What's that look for... Ah!"

Shaddap, I was born with these scary eyes!

Wait, what was with that pause just now?

...Oh, he must have realized all of this was all his fault.

"..."

"..."

"..."

"Oh, uh, well…"

Stare…

"…"

He seemed quite troubled.

Well, I didn't want to pick on him too much.

"Then I will be selling my medicine wholesale to the two shops that are not part of the association, for 80% of the list price. There should be no problem as long as those shops continue selling it at the same price for 20% profit, right?"

"Y-Yes, that's fine, but… you would hardly make any profit that way. There is no need to concede to the harassment and miss out on easy profits like that. This could all be resolved with a little pressure from the military. They wouldn't bother you anymore if I tell them the military and its partners will no longer do business with their three shops."

Hmm, he may have been right, but I didn't want them trying to get back at me, and I didn't care about continuing the business enough to go through all that negativity.

I was worried about someone getting attacked in the night over all of this.

…The concern was mainly for them, though.

I wasn't too keen on seeing Francette or Emile cut a civilian down in front of me.

I had to make sure that wouldn't happen…

"I make enough profit from the box lunch business, so the medicine will just be a service, so as to not inconvenience the customers who have been supporting me. Of course, I'll be supplying those two shops with medicine other than the one for soldier's disease, as well. If they'll accept the deal, that is."

"There's no way they'd refuse such a good deal..."

Yeah, he was right.

"It seems keeping the supplier a secret is how things are done around here, so please keep this between us. If you tell anyone, it'd bring more weirdos my way. If that happens..."

"If that happens...?"

I smiled in response to his question.

"Oh, it's just that no one would be getting any medicine anymore."

Why did he flinch and suddenly move away from me before hearing my response? Huh?

* *

A few days later, right after opening the shop...

"Is the owner here?!"

What happens twice, happens thrice. And this time, the number of complainers had multiplied to three.

I'm the one who wants to multiply, damn it!

"Why did you offer your products to the two other shops and not us?!"

What did they want me to say...?

"What? My medicine shop is no longer in business, just like you all wanted. Did those shops tell you they're getting their products from me?"

"N-No, not exactly..."

"But they're selling the medicine that was being sold here!"

"I wouldn't know anything about that. Besides, I thought trying to force another business to give up their supply route is strictly forbidden? Even if I did close the shop and gave away my supplier to another shop for a high price, what problem is there? And do you think barging in here and demanding that I give you answers isn't a problem?

"How about I go to those two other medicine shops and every other shop in town and tell them what you three are doing, and that you think this is proper behavior as merchants?"

"Wha..."

Of course they wouldn't want that. The other businesses will either frown upon them, no longer work with them, or demand that they give up their suppliers in turn, as well. Whatever their reaction, no one would find this acceptable.

"Last time, however unreasonable your demands, it could have been seen as a proposal from a fellow businessman of the industry, but this is a baseless accusation and threat against a girl in another, unrelated profession. I have a mind to report this to the authorities."

If merchants began taking each other out, there would be less tax revenue to be made. And merchants made far more revenue than the common worker. In addition, this was the royal capital, where taxes would go directly to His Majesty the King.

...In other words, the officials and guards here worked very hard.

"..."

Many pairs of eyes simply stared at the three medicine shop owners in silence. This was right after opening time. In other words, it was the busiest time of day for customers to come in and buy their box meals. Hunters, travelers, military personnel ranking higher than petty officers who lived outside of the barracks, and more.

"Layette's Atelier, Box Meals To Go" had a rather strong clientele.

Those customers stared down the three merchants with an even scarier look.

Their faces turned pale, and they had no choice but to turn tail and run.

"I'm sorry for the wait, everyone. As a token of apology, everyone here will get 20% off of their purchase!"

"Ohh, so generous! You're the best, Kaoru!"

"Flattery isn't going to get you any more of a discount, you know!"

"The only thing that's flat around here is your ches— I mean, nothing!"

The customer must have realized that sounded too cruel even for a joke, and tried to take it back right away.

"You should have just rolled with it as a joke! Feeling bad about it mid-way only made it worse!"

"My bad…"

And so, the shop was filled with laughter.

Chapter 28: The Angel Returns

Five days later…

I woke up and quietly got ready for the day, careful not to wake the still-sleeping Layette. I descended to the first floor and opened the wooden window to find…

"Whoa!"

There was a huge line outside. This wasn't the first time I've had a long queue of customers, but something was off. In previous cases, there was a clear reason for all the customers lining up, like when the store first opened or when we were having a sale. But this time, I couldn't figure out why it was happening. They were quietly standing out there without making a scene, but they each wore a fretful expression with bloodshot eyes.

"Wh-What in the world…"

I was standing there, frozen, when I heard a knock on the door. It was clearly coming from a different door from where the line had been formed.

I removed the bolt and opened the door, then two men burst into the store.

"Kaoru! I need some strong medicine! Ours isn't nearly strong enough!"

"This is an emergency! Please!"

They were the owners of the two medicine shops that weren't a part of the so-called association. Yes, the ones I made a deal with to supply them with my medicine wholesale.

"What happened…?"

"A disease. It seems an epidemic has been going around. It's pretty serious, with the number of patients increasing at a rapid pace. There have even been deaths…"

"What?!"

"Fever, headaches, stomach aches, joint pain, loss of appetite, and fatigue. In some cases, people have died in as quickly as ten days. Even using as many of our strongest herbs as possible before the side effects become too big of a problem has barely helped at all. The court doctor has been working without sleep to no avail. All they could manage to do was close off the royal palace to keep the contamination from getting to the royal family…"

This was bad. I had run a medicine shop at one point, but I had no knowledge of medicine or medical science. It would be far too suspicious to use some elixir that could make a dying old man or woman get up and start dancing, and I couldn't diagnose, let alone figure out, a cure for a disease just by looking at a patient.

The only thing I knew how to diagnose was beriberi. You take a mallet and do that thing where you tap them on the knee with it.

…That wasn't going to do anyone any good.

What to do…

In any case, I had to do something about the long line outside.

"Everyone! I don't have any medicine right now! I'll have to assess the situation and figure out what to do from there, so please return home for today!"

They seemed to understand that it was unreasonable to have such high hopes for a business that had closed down already, and the line dispersed.

Either they were really desperate to come to my shop, or their expectations were just that high… wait, there were still tens of people in line that hadn't left.

"Excuse me, but we still don't have medicine…"

"We're here to buy your box lunches."

Oh…

After selling them some packed meals, I closed the doors, wooden windows, and curtains, then flipped the sign to indicate that we were closed for the day.

I gathered everyone for a meeting. The members were me, the owners of the medicine shops, Layette, who had noticed the commotion and came downstairs, Emile, and Belle. I had them cancel their guild work to stay home. Roland and Francette had appeared out of nowhere, too. It was the all-star cast.

…Oh, but I guess Ed and the others weren't there.

"First, please explain the details of this emergency."

The shop owners proceeded to explain the details as I had requested.

According to them, a highly contagious disease had appeared in a village to the east of the royal capital, and although exit and entry was closed off in an attempt to contain it, sufferers were found in the royal capital a few days ago, and the disease spread quickly.

"Apparently, news of the disease and the quarantine was initially suppressed to avoid chaos. In fact, an official announcement about it still hasn't been made. But there's no hiding it anymore, and the information has been leaked everywhere. So while we're running around trying to find a solution, it's completely unrelated to whatever the authorities are doing about it."

What was this country doing...?

Speed is of the essence in cases like these.

"How foolish. The royal family here seems completely incompetent," Roland commented harshly.

It was probably extra frustrating for him, being royalty himself. A lot of people could end up dying.

As for us, we probably wouldn't be affected by the disease as long as we drank my cure-all medicine. We could simply wait for this epidemic to pass, or move to another country.

Even though I had the funds, I had opted to rent out my store rather than buy it precisely so I could pick up and move whenever I needed. Any interior items I purchased could be thrown into the Item Box. That way, I could reopen my shop in another city with ease.

...Wait, I would never abandon my regulars!

What if people find out who I am? Bring it on! I'll just run away again!

I had made myself a promise on that day.

I'll live the life I want in this world.

I'll be modest, but I won't hold back.

I'll reflect on my mistakes, but I won't have regrets!

"Sorry, everyone. I think we'll have to move again..."

"...Finally. To be honest, our current backstories were a bit hard to deal with..."

Roland gave a forced smile at Francette's words.

Huh? Really? Well, I suppose I should've known.

Sorry, Francette.

"We are at your call."

Ah... Well, I guess Emile and Belle would say that.

"That's okay. I'll follow you wherever you go!"

And I'll protect you, Layette!

Okay, let's do this.

"There you have it. Leave the rest to us."

The shop owners looked at me wide-eyes, not understanding what was happening.

All right, show time! The Angel's Theater was about to begin!

I had the shop owners return home and opened the door to leave the shop. Then I produced a small, thumb-sized whistle from my pocket. I put it up to my lips and...

Fweet, fweet, fweet! Fweet, fweet, fweet! Fweet, fweet, fweet!

Fweet, fweet, fweet! Fweet, fweet, fweet! Fweet, fweet, fweet! Fweet, fweet, fweet! Fweet, fweet, fweet! Fweet, fweet, fweet!

I used all of my lung capacity to blow it as loud as I could. Then, after some time, human figures could be seen running toward us at full speed.

"Number ooone! I was here first, so this job's mine!"

"No, stupid! Did you forget what she told us about the signals? This isn't a normal job... Isn't that right, Lady Kaoru?"

I nodded at the boy who was second to arrive. I would explain once everyone was gathered.

One after another, the children from the orphanage and local street urchins showed up. Actually, the children living in abandoned buildings were technically "homeless" and not street urchins, but that was neither here nor there. These were the children I hired as messengers or to perform miscellaneous tasks for me, in exchange for money or food. I usually issued requests to whoever happened to catch my attention, but we had an arrangement so they would come when I blew the whistle in case there was no one around.

If I blew it once, I would need one person. Two times meant I needed two, and three times meant I needed three. First come, first serve. And if I continued to blow the whistle a bunch of times…

It was the signal for a special assembly.

When this happened, it meant I had a job that required everyone who heard the sound of the whistle. It was the signal for an emergency.

The children who gathered lined up in the order they arrived. They all understood I wouldn't allow any cheating by cutting in line, so there were no arguments.

I explained the contents of the job to all who had gathered.

"Do you know about the epidemic going around the royal capital?"

Some of the relatively older kids nodded.

"I'm going to eradicate it. You're all going to save the royal capital, and this country."

"Whoaaa! No waaay!!!"

I've always paid out their rewards as promised and more. There wasn't a single orphan child or street urchin who would decline work from me or distrust anything I said.

Each child took a potion bottle and silver coin from the bag I had been wearing on my shoulder. The bag was clearly too small to fit everything, but no one seemed to question it. Of course, this included Francette.

Under my order, everyone drank down the potions. Now the children wouldn't catch the disease.

"First, I want you four to go where this person tells you to, and tell people that the owner of Layette's Atelier wants them to gather before the goddess statue at the central plaza before the second morning bell. After that, I want you all to move on to the next task with the other children, which I'm about to explain," I said to four children, pointing toward Roland.

"Roland, tell them where to find the lieutenant colonel, the viscount company commander, and the residences of the two noble houses that visited the shop before. I'm sure you've already done research into the nobles who tried to cause me trouble..."

Roland scratched his head, which I took to mean I was right.

"I want you to go to Salabert Realtors and tell them Layette's Atelier will be closing. Our contract will end today, so please keep the deposit. Join the rest of the group once you're done with that."

This one required the most explanation, so I asked the one who seemed to be the oldest.

Then...

"I want everyone to go around town and spread the word. Tell them that they can get special medicine to cure the epidemic for free. It'll be given out after the second morning bell in front of the goddess statue in the central plaza. Okay, do you have that? All right, go!"

They all went running with a sparkle in their eyes.

"Kaoru, why did you do that?" Francette asked, but the answer was obvious!

"I can't abandon the people of this city after being in their care."

Francette replied, "Yes, I did know you would say that. What I don't understand is, why are you going out of your way to send a messenger to the nobles that caused you trouble?"

Oh, that!

"Whether it's for good or bad, they are acquaintances of mine. If I call for them, they might think it's for a request, and come over thinking they can make money by trading me favors. It would be much harder to call for nobles who I've never met before. I want to use the military and the nobility to spread information as quickly as possible. In other words, I just need them to spread the word, so it doesn't matter if they're good or bad. I need someone who will answer my summons and has a route to quickly send information to other nobles and the royal palace."

"I-I see!"

Francette seemed to finally understand.

Roland probably knew all this from the beginning, but he acted completely disinterested. As expected as the brother of a king… though he was probably higher-spec than His Highness himself.

Now, it was time to put everything in the shop into my Item Box before heading out to the central plaza. I'd be taking the sign too. I could reuse it next time.

* *

When I arrived at the central plaza, there were already quite a lot of people gathered. The four I had asked for still weren't… oh, there were the military officers running toward us. And from the other side, two carriages. Probably the annoying nobles.

All right, the stage was set. It was time to begin. I just needed a high platform…

Yeah, I'm short, so people won't be able to see me or hear my voice by standing at the same height.

Actually, I could take care of the voice issue with this…

Come out, potion in a container like a shoulder megaphone!

Hm, I think I'll stand on the pedestal part of the goddess statue… I mean, Celes's statue.

I hoped nobody would yell at me for being blasphemous.

All right, the military group and nobles were there! I had to start before they started bothering me for an explanation. Time to begin!

"Everyone, thank you for coming. I will now grant you all the medicine for curing the epidemic," I said, standing on the pedestal and speaking loudly using the megaphone.

The gathered crowd quieted down, staring with a blank expression on their faces.

I should probably explain a bit more than that…

"Are you all aware of the terrible disease spreading across the royal capital?"

Some of them knew, while others were hearing about it for the first time or had suspected it but weren't sure. Not everyone had known about it, but they all seemed to figure out what was going on by how the people around them were acting. And, gradually, an anxious clamor began to spread.

"Yes, it's a dangerous disease that has even resulted in death!"

The crowd grew more restless.

"Stop! What are you plotting?!"

The lieutenant colonel rushed up to stop me, but Roland and Francette blocked his path. Emile and Belle stopped the viscount company commander, as well.

Yeah, I expected they would try to interrupt. There was a reason there had been no official announcement, despite the news being widespread already. Because once someone pulled the trigger, there would be panic, chaos, and possibly a riot. And I was seemingly acting as an agitator.

However!

"I will now distribute a specific remedy for this disease! If you drink it, it will protect you from getting infected, and those who have already contracted it will be cured. There's plenty to go around—many times more than the total population of the royal capital—so please, line up in a calm, orderly manner, because there's plenty to go around. Or else..."

Then I created a "nitroglycerin-like thing" a few meters above the ground between me and the crowd.

Boom!

"You will be struck down by the wrath of the Goddess!"

The noisy crowd instantly fell quiet.

I began chanting strange incantations into the megaphone, conscious of the fact that everyone's attention was focused on me.

"My friend, the Goddess Celestine, grant us salvation from this wicked disease! Come forth, Medicine Pot of Miracles!!!"

Then a miniature goddess statue, about two meters in height, suddenly appeared at the base of the goddess statue. A tiled pot was held up at its right shoulder, where a white fluid poured out. The fluid poured down toward the mini goddess statue's feet, where it seemed to vanish as it was drained at the base.

Yes, it was being returned and recirculated into the pot. Who knows what would happen if such a suspicious fluid was endlessly poured into the city sewers? It would be pretty bad if the mice living down there turned into super mice or something.

The crowd still didn't utter a word and gulped audibly. A goddess statue had suddenly appeared out of nowhere. White fluid poured out endlessly from the pot that the statue was holding.

A strange girl. An explosion of divine judgment. The royal capital's crisis. The Goddess's protection.

"Uooohhh!!!"

Suddenly, the crowd erupted in cheers.

I continued shouting in the megaphone in an attempt to control the crowd.

"Quiet down! Stay calm! The medicine will flow without end, so there's no need to rush! Prioritize the children, the elderly, and those who are already sick, and patiently wait your turn. Do you want to act shamefully in front of your family and friends? Do you want to incur the wrath of the Goddess?"

It would be an absolute disaster if the crowd all rushed forward at once. In order to prevent this, I had given them a feeling of security by telling them there was an endless supply of medicine, and planted in them fear of the Goddess's divine punishment.

No one would doubt the existence of divine punishment after witnessing such a miracle. In fact, they had just seen it with their own eyes.

"I want the lieutenant colonel and the company commander to inform the royal palace and military. And don't forget about the guard regiment and the royal sentries. You two, go around the noble district and inform the other nobles. They wouldn't listen if a commoner was to spread the news. Let's see… you may tell them a friend of Celestine has just appeared."

I changed up my speech pattern a bit to sound more authoritative. The two nobles simply stood there with mouths agape, but the officers were on top of it. An officer in the military couldn't survive if they were dumbfounded by every unexpected situation. They saluted and got ready to run off…

"Oh, wait!"

I called out to them, then grabbed two potion bottles out of thin air. Their eyes widened, as well as the rest of the crowd.

"It's the same medicine as that one. Drink it."

The two drank it down without hesitation. Then I grabbed two cloth bags out of the air.

"There are twelve bottles each inside. Have the king drink it. We can't have His Majesty and the ministers lining up with the rest of the crowd, can we?"

They took the bags wordlessly, bowed their heads, then ran off toward the royal palace.

...Huh?

"Why are you two not going?" I asked the two nobles, who were still standing there.

"W-Well, we were hoping for some medicine as well..."

Oh, right!

"Here!"

I grabbed two bottles out of thin air, and handed them one each. Once they drank them...

"...Why are you still waiting?"

"U-Um, the medicine bag..."

Ah.

"You won't be getting one. The regular nobles will have to line up normally with the rest of the people."

"Whaaat!"

They were still taking their sweet time, but they ran off immediately after I glared at them.

Fear the demon eyes! ...Hey, shut up!

"Now, once you've formed a line, move forward promptly but without rushing! One sip of the medicine will be enough. Please also put some in a container for the people who weren't able to come here due to age or sickness!"

"Huh…?"

Ah, judging by the reaction from some of them, I could tell they were up to no good…

"Also… it would be pointless to try to take a lot of it to save for later, because this medicine won't work for any other illness, its efficacy will expire in a day, and you can get it here for free. And if you're petty enough to do such a thing, who knows what your family and friends would think… Even if you need some for your family, one cup will be enough for ten people or so. You would even be fine with less. So keep moving and don't hold up the line! Drinking one scoop from your hand will be enough!"

All right, things were finally moving along! I was set for now.

Layette squeezed my right hand.

She was worried about me…

There was no turning back now…

But I had no choice. Judging from what the two medicine shop owners told me, the disease was spreading at an alarmingly rapid rate. It was probably moving far quicker than the plague, typhus, or cholera.

Even a little bit of delay in its treatment would result in it spreading throughout the kingdom, and eventually the entire continent. It would all happen in the blink of an eye. And I had no way to tell diseases apart.

Of course not! What do you expect from an ex-newbie office lady?!

I couldn't diagnose the plague or typhus, and I knew nothing about the causes, traits, or treatments for any disease. The only thing I did know was that beriberi diagnosis method where you tap your knee. And selling medicine in my shop wouldn't have helped. Only people who were relatively well-off would have gone out to purchase medicine.

Orphans, street urchins, the homeless, and even normal citizens often relied on free folk remedies rather than purchasing medicine. There were some who wouldn't buy medicine even if it was really cheap or even free. Then it would have all been pointless, and conversely, if everyone in the royal capital came barging into my store, I wouldn't have been able to handle that, either.

So I had to go somewhere spacious and give it out for free, with a method where everyone would be rushing in all at once, but while avoiding panic and preventing people from fighting over the medicine or the nobles and royals trying to keep it for themselves… Only the Goddess or the Angel could fulfill all those conditions.

In other words, it was checkmate.

I didn't even know what the disease was called. But if I went around giving out medicine that could cure any disease, the world would go on a witch hunt… no, an Angel hunt. I'm no masochist, so I had to pass on that.

And so, I had the convenient Goddess-branded Potion Factory (named by me) resolve everything. This was the result that came of it.

[Potion that cures and creates antibodies for any epidemic disease going around in the royal capital right now with just a low dose and loses its effectiveness if it's not drunk in twenty-four hours after being scooped, go inside a small container shaped like a goddess statue with an endless generation/circulation system and come out!]

That's cheating, you say? It's fine, I'm the one who makes the rules.

Despite the massive crowd of people gathered, each person took very little time.

Some people took it upon themselves to organize the lines, leading the people so that they moved in from the side instead of all coming directly from the front.

Smart! It would take more time if everyone went to the front, because each person would need to stop, scoop, drink, then move aside, but they would only need to stop for a moment this way.

Well done.

The volunteer workers seemed very happy, and I could even see a glimmer in their eyes. I mean, they were helping the Angel, so they must have felt like they'd become servants of the Goddess.

Of course they're happy.

It seemed I could leave the rest to them without worry.

Then, after some time, *they* arrived. Yup, of course. *Them.* The military. Most of them were foot soldiers, but there were some cavalry, as well.

...And a crowd of nobles.

"Out of the way, commoners! The miracle medicine belongs to the house of Marquess Sessdor..."

Boom!

"A-Ahhh!"

As the noble rode his carriage through the rows of citizens, toward the goddess statue, I gently gifted him the nitroglycerin-like thing. The roof of his carriage was blown off, and his two horses sat down on the spot out of fear.

Horses are quite timid creatures. A single crow or a shadow flying by in front of them could cause them to stop or run away. Maybe they opted to sit down because they couldn't run away while also drawing the carriage.

The noble in the carriage shrank down and covered his head with both hands, perhaps to protect his head from the falling shards of the roof or because he was cowering in fear.

"Fool! It seems you don't value your life, to oppose the will of the Goddess like this… Then, as you wish, I'll grant you a swift death. That way, you won't need to worry about the disease anymore."

My voice, amplified by the shoulder megaphone, spread throughout the plaza. The sound was high quality without any distortion… well, of course it would be. It was a special order straight from the Goddess's workshop.

All right, the nobles and the army had stopped in place. At the front of the group was… the lieutenant colonel.

"Behold, the miracle of the Goddess!"

Then I created another mini goddess statue.

One, two… it didn't make much difference now. So I decided to prioritize making an impactful impression to the nobles and army.

"The soldiers are to line up at this second goddess statue and drink the medicine. Afterward, under your commander's orders, you will cooperate with the sentries to maintain order in the royal capital, distribute medicine to the sick, and spread the word that the disease has been overcome. Anyone who drinks the medicine will be immune to this epidemic. As for the nobles… you will line up normally behind the rest of the citizens."

The soldiers roared in jubilation, and their superior officers quickly began forming lines.

I had to give it to the military. They moved in an orderly fashion, and formed rows quickly and efficiently. Though I could hear grumblings from the nobles…

"There is no difference between nobles and commoners before the Goddess. That's a distinction humans have made by themselves. If you don't like it, feel free to leave without the medicine."

They shut up and got in line pretty quickly after that.

Oh, it looked like some of the nobles had their servants bring containers instead of lining up themselves. It seemed they had gotten my message. I guess those two I sent off to spread the word had done their job well.

But why did they go through the trouble of coming in person? Maybe they wanted to see the miracle for themselves, or they were plotting to take the goddess statue…

"Kaoru, I mean, Lady Angel…"

It was the lieutenant colonel. He had ridden over on his horse.

"Kaoru is fine. It weirds me out when you address me that way…"

"I can't… well, I suppose you're right. That's the kind of person you are…"

I was glad he seemed to agree.

There were several unfamiliar faces. Judging by the way they were acting as equals to the lieutenant colonel, they must have been the leaders of the other battalions. Though, it didn't look like all nine of them were there…

"So, Kaoru, what are you planning on doing after this?"

Yeaaah, that was the question. There wasn't much I could do now. Then I'd have to take care of things properly.

"I'm going east."

"East?"

"Yes, toward the village to the east, where this epidemic is believed to have started.

If I don't contain it there, the disease could spread to places other than the royal capital, resulting in a real disaster…"

The lieutenant colonel had a grave look on his face upon hearing this.

"That village has already been contained. People are prohibited from exit and entry, and they've been quarantined until the disease passes."

...In other words, they're waiting for the villagers to die as they're trapped in the village? Or were they going to disinfect the entire village by setting fire to it?

Not on my watch!

I turned toward the people who had volunteered to organize the lines.

"I must go to a village to save those who are suffering from disease. So, please handle things here until the statues have fulfilled their duty."

"You can count on us, my lady!!!"

They had been given a task by the Angel of the Goddess. Such an honor was unheard of. Five men raised their arms proudly, eyes glimmering with purpose.

"Once the soldiers are done, please form a second line and use that statue for the citizens as well. Now, I leave the rest to you."

With that, I leapt down from the pedestal of the goddess statue. The sea of people parted before me.

Who am I, Moses?!

Well, I doubted there was anyone who would try to stand in my way. After all, I was the Angel of the Goddess, going out to save a dying village from an epidemic.

"...I'll lead the way," the lieutenant colonel offered suddenly.

Hmm, what to do...

There were going to be a lot of soldiers over there anyway, so there was no point in sending him away. And I didn't know where this village was.

At this point, it was meaningless to try and keep secrets.

The soldiers at the village might try to stop me, so it could be more convenient to have a high-ranking officer with me...

As I thought about it, the lieutenant colonel whispered in my ear, "Please, if I'm granted the task of guiding the Angel of the Goddess, it would help my career in the future..."

Ahh, I got it. That made sense. I decided I would let him play the part. He had helped me with a bunch of things in the past, so I decided to repay him.

Let's see, the lieutenant colonel's name was... wait, I don't remember! I always called him the lieutenant colonel or battalion commander instead of his name...

Oh, well.

"Commander of the royal army's second battalion, I ask you to act as my guide to the village. Lead me there, so that we may save the villagers!"

"You honor me! I, Nevas von Vonsas, third son of the house of Count Vonsas and the second battalion leader of the royal army, will see this through, even if it costs my life!"

He was really into it.

...Though I was one to talk.

No, I was just playing it up because the people would be more likely to listen to me if I acted all mighty. Besides, having it known that the Angel has a grand attitude would distance that persona from the usual me, making it harder for people to figure out we're one in the same. I had put some thought into it, after all.

But, I had to say, the lieutenant colonel really knew how to put himself out there, stating his full name and everything. I was thoroughly impressed. He talked loud and clear, so his voice carried pretty well. For those who couldn't hear him, my shoulder megaphone amplified my own voice, so the advertisement was effective enough.

Now, it was time to get out of there.

We made our way through the crowd of people that had parted to either side, the lieutenant colonel in the lead.

He was riding on horseback, while the rest of us walked.

Boo hoo.

He offered to bring a carriage, but I declined. If I had agreed, Ed would have been furious, being out of the picture for so long. So, we went to the stable where Ed was to round up everyone else.

"*Took you long enough! We've been waiting forever!*" all five horses, including Ed, complained at once.

Apparently, they were bored out of their minds.

Sorry about that...

I decided to keep them at a stable with a pasture next time.

I'll even come visit once in a while, so please forgive me.

I climbed on top of Ed with Layette in my arms, then we were off. After distancing ourselves from the royal capital, where there was no one around to see...

"Come out, chariot!"

A miniature carriage appeared out of nowhere, and the lieutenant colonel stared with his mouth hanging open. But he quickly regained his composure. I mean, he's already seen worse.

After tethering the carriage to Ed, I put Layette on board and climbed in after her.

"Let's go!"

Goodbye, royal capital! I probably wasn't going to return after this. Though, I may pass through, quietly, the next time I return to Balmore.

Yes, quietly! No way was I going to come back as the Angel with a flourish of trumpets!

In any case, I had to get to the village to the east.

"There are a lot of lives on the line. I'm counting on you, Ed!"

"Leave it to me, missy!"

Excited for his time to shine, Ed took the lead in pulling the carriage along with the four other horses. The lieutenant colonel's horse followed behind us. Oh, I guess Ed really wasn't just a normal horse…

There was an awkward smile on the lieutenant colonel's face, and his horse watched us with disbelief.

…I think I'll give him a potion later. Not to the lieutenant colonel, of course, but to his horse.

*　　*

We arrived at the eastern village before dusk. As soon I saw the village up ahead, I put the carriage into the Item Box and got onto Ed, with Layette in my arms. We continued forward at a walking pace, and as we veered from the main road and toward a path leading to the village, we spotted several soldiers there.

"Stop!" the soldiers ordered, and I complied.

They could surely see the lieutenant colonel in the back, but they couldn't just let me go without stopping me. Their eyes wandered toward the lieutenant colonel with a troubled look.

"Entry is prohibited beyond this point. Go back to the main road and toward the next village. You should get there before it gets dark."

Yeah, he seemed like a good, diligent soldier.

But I refuse!

"I run a medicine shop. I've heard about the epidemic and prepared a specific medicine for it. I've already succeeded in stopping the spread of the disease in the royal capital. All that's left is to cure the afflicted in this village."

"I-Is that so?!"

The soldier surely didn't want to close off the village and let its inhabitants die miserably. Upon hearing my words, his face broke into a smile. He glanced at the lieutenant colonel, who gave a deep nod, and his faint smile turned into a full grin.

"Go on through! And please, save the villagers!"

I wasn't sure if they were familiar with the gesture, but I gave a thumbs up and made my way into the village. Before we entered the village, I saw the soldier closing off the path again. How prudent...

But I supposed it was proper procedure to double check for safety-related concerns. As I approached, a soldier called out to me.

"How did you get in here?!"

Right, there was a soldier blocking the entrance, so I couldn't blame him for being surprised to find someone there. This guy was probably there to make sure people weren't leaving the village, instead. Well, if he's asking how we got there, I had to answer.

"We came by chariot!"

The soldier had a blank expression on his face.

"...Chariot?"

Don't ask!

"She's from a medicine shop. She brought medicine for the epidemic. Let us through!" the lieutenant colonel's exasperated voice called out from behind, and we were able to go through without incident. He should have done that in the first place! And why was he in the back when he's supposed to be leading us?

So useless…

Well, we were able to get in the village, so I guess it was fine.

There were no soldiers around once we were inside. But I guess that made sense, considering they wouldn't want to get sick. In fact, there was no one around at all. It seemed everyone was cooped up in their homes.

So, it was time to do my thing. I took the megaphone I had on my shoulder from back at the royal capital and…

"People of the village, I bring you medicine for your illness! One sip, and you'll be cured! For those of you who aren't able to move, please have your family members get it for you! For those without family members, please call out and I'll come to you!"

With a small village like this, there was no need for me to go over the top, like I did in the royal capital. All I had to do was hand people a potion bottle normally.

Some time after I made my announcement, the doors of several houses rattled open, and people began coming outside. Perhaps they were too sick to go outside, or hiding for fear of getting infected. Probably both.

Oh, but maybe they had been instructed to stay indoors.

They may not have fully trusted my words yet, but an infected person with worsening symptoms had nothing left to lose. Besides, it was highly unlikely for someone to visit a place quarantined by soldiers just to trick people.

The villagers began approaching us, slowly and cautiously. The doors of the other houses were also slightly ajar, with many eyes peeking from the openings.

Well, I figured I only needed a couple guinea pigs. There was no need for everyone to try it at once.

My voice, amplified by the speaker, seemed to reach them well enough, and even the soldier by the main road had walked over to see what I was doing. I figured they had been ordered not to get any closer than where they already were. If they happened to get infected, they would spread the illness to everyone else in the royal capital. Not to mention, the soldiers would be the first ones to fall victim if it did spread. This meant they had to obey their orders, no matter what, even if they wanted to help the villagers.

Ah!

I was forgetting something. I pretended to grab a potion out of my bag, and…

"Belle, give this to the soldiers for me. Tell them it's medicine that'll keep them from getting sick."

"Okay!"

I'd feel pretty bad if the soldiers ended up a source of infection even after I'd cured all the villagers, resulting in all the cities and villages getting infected except the royal capital, where I had already given out a bunch of medicine.

…Huh, the soldiers took the medicine from Belle, but ended up putting it into their pockets after deliberating over what to do. I suppose it wasn't impossible for it to have been poison, used to take out the soldiers so I could rile up the villagers to march into the royal capital. Even with the lieutenant colonel there, some younger soldiers wouldn't recognize a superior officer from another unit, and anyone could get hold of a military uniform. It wasn't unusual for soldiers to listen only to their direct superiors when carrying out important missions. I had no problem with them waiting to decide until they saw the results for themselves.

"…Is it true? Can this illness really be cured?"

A villager finally approached me, glaring at me suspiciously as he asked.

Well, I suppose I did look like a child to these people. I reached into my bag and pulled out a potion, then presented it to him.

"Drink it."

The man still had some strength left in him, but it was clear to see the sickness had weakened him significantly. He opened the bottle, then drained its contents with desperation.

"Ugh…"

"Wh-What's the matter?!"

"It tastes good…"

The villagers slumped their shoulders.

Then the man who drank the potion said, "My body feels lighter… and I think my head feels clearer too…"

It was probably from his fever being reduced.

The medicine had the effect of exterminating pathogens and returning the body to its normal state, so his body temperature would go back to normal, but his diminished energy wouldn't recover, which explained why he was still feeling woozy. I added the effect to cure abnormalities because I didn't want them to die before making a recovery just because if I had simply killed off the pathogen, but it would have been far too unnatural and creepy if they had immediately recovered after taking the medicine.

They'd regain their appetites once they got their strength back, so this should be good enough.

The man's cheeks still looked a bit sunken, but he was far less pale than before, and it was clear to see he felt better after drinking the potion. After seeing this, the villagers all presented their hands to me at once.

"Give us some medicine, too!"

"All right, all right. There's plenty of potions to go around for everyone, so please stay calm and drink slowly!" I said, as I created more potions, pretending to pull them out of my bag, and handed them to the villagers, who opened them and immediately drained their contents.

"...I feel better."

"My chest doesn't feel tight anymore..."

"My stomach pain is gone..."

Stomach pain and chest tightness? The other medicine shop owners mentioned symptoms like those, but what kind of illness could it be? Maybe the plague, or typhus?

But it wasn't necessarily going to be a type of disease that exists on Earth, and there was no way for me to tell them apart anyway, so there was no point in me trying to figure out what it was called anyway.

As I thought about this...

"Let me have some for my ma and son!"

"For my parents and little sister!"

Five of the villagers reached out again for more medicine. I pretended to get more out of the bag again, and handed them potions I created on the spot.

Before I knew it, many people were emerging from their houses to gather there. They didn't have enough energy to run over, but they were hurrying to the best of their abilities.

I guess I didn't need to do the old Angel act this time around. Just so you know, I wasn't doing that because I wanted to! I mean, I was getting a little carried away once I got into it, but who wouldn't?

I'm only human, after all.

Kaoru.

But what was the point of playing Angel for a village with just 200 to 300 people when I didn't need to?

If it wasn't necessary, it was better not to do it. Better for my own mental health, that is.

Though, really, I was pretty sure people had started to catch on by now. I was pulling out way more potions than it would be possible to fit in my little bag.

*　　*

Meals were being prepared in the center of the village. Despite having been cured of their illnesses, many of the villagers were still too feeble to prepare food or eat, and so they were all hungry.

Since it was inefficient for everyone to cook their own food in their own homes, they wanted to celebrate their village having avoided certain doom by having a communal meal together.

They wouldn't be able to recover their strength without eating something nutritious. Just staving off hunger wasn't enough. And so, they would make hotchpotch, which was full of nutritious food and easy to digest.

The village chief wanted to have a festival, but I shot that idea down real quick. People would die if we were to do that.

I mean, some of them could barely walk straight, and seemed to be just managing to hold on. I made those people eat before waiting for the full meal, and mixed some weakened healing potion into their food just so they'd survive.

If we threw a festival in this state, things would get out of hand with people getting drunk and rowdy, and someone could actually die. Everyone may have seemed to be okay now, but their negative conditions had simply been removed, and it didn't mean they had their full vitality back. There have been many deaths from this epidemic already. Why risk adding more to that list of casualties?

Yes, I do get the importance of mourning the lives lost and celebrating those who had survived, and that having a festival would be a good way to show appreciation to the Goddess and process everything, but that could wait until everyone was fully recovered.

"How much time do you think we have?"

"I can't be certain, but I'd say if we left tomorrow afternoon, we should arrive late at night. The soldier that left earlier will arrive at the royal capital before dawn and report first thing in the morning. Then they'll discuss the news in the morning meeting, followed by dispatching someone to confirm the news. A carriage will be sent to receive you, but the Temple of the Goddess will butt in and argue, delaying the departure to the afternoon."

"Ahhh..."

One of the soldiers that was standing guard at the village had gone to the royal capital to report the situation. They couldn't enter the village or interact with the inhabitants, so things like well water, food, or fodder for animals couldn't be obtained from there. Since they couldn't take care of horses, there weren't any there. This meant the soldier had to travel on foot, which would take some time.

I was asked if they could use Ed or my other horses, but I obviously declined. I might have made an exception for an emergency, but there was no need to rush when the crisis was already resolved. Besides, I wanted to buy more time, so there was no reason for me to help. I couldn't just leave Ed, either.

"Then we'll have until tomorrow evening at the latest..."

I've already told the lieutenant colonel that we'll be leaving this place. He really tried to stop us, but after thoroughly explaining what would happen if we stayed, and how much I would hate it, he finally seemed to understand. I was sure he'd have tried to take me back to the royal capital if I was a regular girl, but it seemed defying the will of the Angel was a bit too much of a hurdle for him.

...Being the Angel sure was convenient.

And so, I wanted to get out of there before the men from the royal capital arrived, but there was something I had to take care of first. I had asked that question earlier to try to figure out how much time I had.

Hmm, one whole day. Would I make it in time...?

The thing I had to take care of was, of course, to figure out the reason the disease broke out in the first place. A powerful epidemic had suddenly occurred in some ordinary village. Did a pathogen spontaneously mutate that way by chance? The possibility wasn't zero, but it would be better to confirm. I had nothing to lose by trying, so I might as well use the time I had to give it a shot.

Once everyone was nice and full, the village chief gathered all the key people there upon my request. Of course, no one had any alcohol, so they were all sober.

"I'm about to ask a very important question. This involves the future of this village, so please think about it carefully before answering."

They nodded tensely, seeing my serious expression and words after they had just managed to avoid their demise.

I spread a piece of paper out in front of them, then drew a big circle onto it.

"Let's say this is a map of this entire village. Please indicate which houses have had deaths occur."

"S-Sure..."

They didn't seem to quite understand what was going on, but did as I asked.

Even as I looked at what they had drawn, there didn't seem to be any significant deviations.

"Were there any common factors between those who had passed away?"

The village chief answered my question.

"Ah, well, I suppose they were the children and the elderly, those who weren't too strong to begin with, and the ones who were the first to get infected..."

Ahh, I'm so stupid! Of course!

"I'm sorry, but please stop writing what I requested earlier and show me which houses were infected first instead."

With that, I pulled out a new piece of paper and drew another big circle. The villagers went to work again without a word of complaint.

"The first ones to get sick were Mark, Kiara, and Joey..."

"Martha and Joshua, too..."

Oh, I almost forgot.

"Excuse me, but please divide the time frames into ten and number them from one through ten."

Since they didn't understand the reason for this process, I had to be more specific with my instructions.

All right, they're making good progress...

"Hmm..."

"Did you figure something out?" Roland asked, despite being pretty quiet until that point.

"Hmm, a lot of the early cases are concentrated around here, but that could just be because they lived near the first victims..."

"Then it sounds like there isn't much of a point in checking the concentrated regions."

He wasn't wrong, but maybe there was a hint in there somewhere...

There was another concentrated region off in a different spot, but that was likely because someone contracted it early and it spread around from that person. I thought something would become more clear if we drew it out, but maybe we needed a professional to look at it, instead of amateurs like us.

Hmm...

"The valley!"

"Ah!"

I bent backward in surprise as the village chief suddenly shouted.

"The thing that the early victims all had in common was the valley! The early cases concentrated here are on the valley side of the village, where all the hunters live. The hunters go through the forest and toward the valley to hunt wild animals. The sporadic early victims you see here and then Kiara, Martha, and Weidt. They were either housemaids who dyed textiles at the valley, or youths who occasionally went out to catch fish. The valley must be the source of all this!"

Wow! He understood perfectly why I had them draw this out, utilized his knowledge of the residents to analyze the information and had come to the logical conclusion! Just who was this geezer?!

...Oh, right. The village chief.

"Incredible, Chief! I've heard you were known as a prodigy as a child..."

"Hm, I suppose they did call me that once upon a time."

Ugh! That annoying smug face from getting his butt kissed by the villagers…

But, well, what he said was reasonable, and I wouldn't have known about the valley or who goes there if it wasn't for him. He deserved the credit.

"Well done, Mr. Village Chief! I'll go investigate the valley tomorrow, so may I have someone healthy accompany me as a guide?"

"Certainly! You're the savior of this village, so we'll do what we can to help. I'll have one of the hunters who hasn't gotten sick guide you, so please take care of this."

Afterward, we joined the village chief at his home. It was pretty common for small villages without inns like this one to have visitors stay at the village chief's house. The reason the chief's house was bigger and nicer than the rest of the villagers wasn't because he got to live luxuriously due to his status… well, maybe there was some of that. But even there, there were reasons for things being the way they were.

The soldiers? They said they were going to take turns napping. That was just the nature of their jobs, so that was that.

I thought more soldiers would have been sent from the royal capital every few days to replace them, but according to the villagers, they only sent carriages with water and food, while the soldiers stayed in place. It must've been to prevent people in the royal capital from getting sick.

These poor soldiers…

Maybe I'd do something nice for them later.

We left the royal capital before noon and it started to get dark as the sun went down. We were okay on food because we'd eaten at the communal meal earlier, so I decided to hash out the plans for tomorrow at the village chief's house.

Whatever happened, we'd be leaving this place by tomorrow evening. When we did, I guess I was just going to tell the villagers not to let visitors enter the village, no matter what.

All of the villagers drank the medicine, so they were already fully immune to the disease, but I wanted to discover the cause, if possible.

Besides, there was a chance it could spread somewhere besides the royal capital. The people of this village only went to the royal capital and back, but visitors wouldn't necessarily be heading only to the royal capital. And I'm sure there were people who went to other cities from the royal capital after the disease spread there.

It was possible that it may have already spread elsewhere. Maybe it was spreading village to village, city to city, even now…

I'm only one person. I can't go around every city and village. It would be impossible to stop it from spreading while trying to play catch-up from behind.

Replicate myself using potions? That'd be way too creepy! And if I did that, I wasn't sure if there would be a way to reverse it. I was afraid each of the copies would start claiming to be the original and killing each other. Ya know, that "cogito ergo sum" thing I read about in a manga.

Eeek!

"What's wrong, Big Sis Kaoru? You don't look so good."

Layette sounded concerned as she spoke to me.

"Something wrong, Kaoru? You've got a scary look in your eyes."

"Oh, no. I'm okay… And Roland?

"Shut it!"

*　　*

The next day, we departed for the valley with a hunter from the village guiding us.

"Lieutenant Colonel, you can head back to the royal capital now if you'd like. You've already fulfilled your duty in leading us here."

"I can't just turn back now! His Majesty would be angry with me if I don't see this through to the end!"

"Ah, right..."

And so the eight of us, which included me, the lieutenant colonel, and the hunter guiding us, all began making our way into the forest. There was actually a beaten path for us to follow, though.

We were still some distance away from the valley, but I decided to put it on at this point. Yes, I'm talking about the glasses-type destination detector I thought of last night. The left lens had a PPI scope (Plan Position Indicator scope: plane coordinates display screen) and the right lens pointed out the position of the destination with arrows and dots.

Oh, actually, let me rephrase that. It's a glasses-type destination detector shaped potion container. There's a potion inside the part that secures the device to my face. And I could still see what's in front of me while wearing it, though it did make it a bit more difficult.

It's used for finding things, so I decided to call it a Searcher. It doesn't read the opponent's power level or anything, so I decided against calling it that other name. I already showed it to the others last night, so no one was surprised to see it.

Even though the hunter was seeing it for the first time, he had already seen the infinite potions popping out of my bag and their effects, so it wasn't anything to be surprised by at this point.

I had set the Searcher to find the pathogen that had caused this disease. Even if I couldn't find it right away, there was no need to rush. Whenever we got to the valley in question, I could just increase the search range from there.

For now, I just needed it to ensure that we didn't miss out on anything important.

But wait... what's this?

There were a bunch of blips on the left side of the PPI scope. And since they were close by, I could see each individual point moving around clearly.

They were moving far too fast to be microbes. And their movement speed and directions were too erratic to have been blown around by the wind. Plus, the points themselves were too big.

They were infected animals!

This was bad. If the disease could spread to humans from animals, there was no telling when someone other than the people in the village or royal capital, who haven't had the medicine, could get infected.

And if someone did get infected, it could spread again in some other city. Not only that, but infected animals caught by the hunters of this or any other village would be sold to local merchants. Those would be delivered to not only the royal capital, but to all the other cities. If the animal meat is eaten without being fully heated to kill off the microbes...

In any case, we had to get to the valley.

And so, we eventually arrived at the valley. There was a small stream with clear water there. It was likely a watering spot for the animals in the area. So, the hunters also likely hunted here too.

There were lots of points at the stream lighting up on my detector, but there weren't any animals there that I could see.

...Maybe they were small animals, like mice?

All right, I'll extend the range and… What the?!

They seemed to be moving erratically when viewed close range, but when I extended the range, I could see the whole image more clearly. Their minute movements were no longer visible, and instead, the PPI scope showed their movement as a whole. There was a clear center, and the light points became less concentrated as they went further from the middle.

It was spreading out in a radial pattern. This had to be the source of the outbreak.

The Searcher's so useful!

"We're heading toward what seems to be the source. I don't know what we'll find there, so be careful, everyone! Roland, keep your eyes on Layette. Everyone else, stay alert!"

I had to make sure Layette was safe, and I suppose Roland too, since he was royalty. Belle and Emile were fully-fledged hunters already, so they could protect themselves. The hunter's a professional too, so I figured he could handle himself.

Though, really, I didn't think we'd be in too much danger. The villagers hadn't been exposed to any danger besides the disease until this point, after all, but it wouldn't hurt to be cautious. It was possible an animal that had become sick could turn violent or something.

We stayed vigilant as we made our way toward the center of the points on the detector, and as we reached the most concentrated area…

"The heck is this?!"

We found something strange. A squishy thing that was about three to four meters in diameter.

…Thing? No, there wasn't an actual object there.

It was like the dimension itself was writhing, after being all twisted around…

From there, a sort of miasma was leaking out with small, mouse-like creatures coming out periodically.

"There it iiis!" I shouted, but I had no idea what it was.

It didn't seem like it could be cut with a sword, and I felt like something terrible would happen if I touched it. Yeah, we definitely shouldn't touch that thing. Let sleeping dogs lie, as they say.

"Kaoru, what is that warped thing…?"

Ah.

I realized what it was when Francette asked me the question. This wasn't a job for humans. It wasn't something any human could handle. So what should I do?

That's right, I'd just call someone who could handle it.

"Potion inside that crystal ball shaped container, come out!"

And so, a crystal ball appeared between my palms as I put them together.

"Activate, emergency calling device!"

The next moment, the crystal ball emitted a brilliant light, and a sphere of light appeared in the air immediately after. That sphere of light began to take shape, eventually turning into the form of a beautiful girl. Yes, the Goddess Celestine had descended.

"Where is the distortion?!"

Celes said the same exact line as she did four years ago.

"Kaoru? Oh, this isn't about a distortion? What is it?"

"There."

"Huh?"

Celes had a blank look on her face. She seemed to think I had called her for some other reason using that sketchy crystal for emergency use.

But…

"There. I thought that might be the 'distortion' you've been looking for…"

"Huh? What? Whaaat?! Ah, you're right! It's a distortion!!!" Celes let out a shout of surprise.

Meanwhile, everyone else stood in an even more shocked state, their mouths agape. Even Francette and Roland, who had already seen her four years ago…

"Get back! Everyone, please stand further away!"

No one even reacted to Celes's panicked voice.

"We need to run! Follow me if you don't want your body to get ripped apart!"

Getting torn into pieces while getting rid of a distortion once was enough! I ran with Layette in my arms, and everyone seemed to finally come to as they followed after me. They must have realized how serious this was after seeing how even the Goddess and her Angel were panicking.

But Celes…

Did you really need to do this in such a hurry?

It'd been a long time since that thing was created, so couldn't she just wait a few minutes longer? At least until we got to a safe distance?

No, there was no point in saying this. This was Celes we're talking about. Yes, because it's Celes.

Damn it!

Roland took Layette from my arms as he ran past me. As expected of royalty, he knew what to do even when flustered. I had to give it to him.

...Though he kept running on, leaving me completely behind.

I mean, that was totally fine! I'd rather Layette be saved than all of us die together.

Emile was leading Belle by her hand... staying directly behind me. They were probably thinking of using their own bodies as shields to protect me, even though they could easily outrun me...

Sheesh, those two knuckleheads...

And Francette was protecting them from behind as well. Argh, why was everyone so dumb?!

The lieutenant colonel and hunter? They're waaay in the front! I guess they didn't want to get involved in heavenly conflicts. But they're the normal ones!

This was bad, I was reaching my limit because of my lack of athleticism...

M-My leg cramped up!

Baaam! I fell flat on the ground, and...

Oof, oof!

I felt something hit my back twice. Belle and Emile went down with me? No, they were using their bodies as shields to protect me!

Y-You dummies!

"Here it comes!" Francette called out, and I felt another impact.

Urgh!

Yeah, that was Francette stacking on top of us.

...I knew it.

Then a heavy impact came over us.

*　　*

"I thought we were done for..."

Belle and Emile said as they rose to their feet. Ugh, I thought they were going to crush me to death!

As for Francette and Celes... Oh, there they were.

"Please explain, why didn't you wait until Kaoru got somewhere safe?!"

Gyaaa! Why was Fran scolding Celes?! Celes may seem mild-mannered, but she's pretty short-tempered and humans are like ants to her. It was just that sometimes she felt like helping when a lot of humans were in danger of dying at once. So unless she has some interest in you like she does with me, she'd just squish...

"I-I'm sorry..."

...H-Huh?

"Kaoru is in a mortal's body right now, so her body could be destroyed if you do something so reckless!"

"Y-You're right..."

Whoa, their conversation was miraculously meshing together...

"She's your friend, so you should be more considerate..."

"Yes..."

Huh, she must have been acting docile because it was concerning me.

"As a fellow goddess, you must learn to be more like Kaoru..."

Gyaaaaaa!

"Let's just leave it at that, okay, Fran?!"

"Mmg..."

I swiftly ran toward Francette and covered her mouth. We were treading on thin ice. Celes could lose it any moment now.

"So, Celes, I wanted to ask about this distortion..."

I really did want to know more about it, of course. But for now, my main objective was to distract Celes.

"Oh, yes! Thank you, Kaoru! You really helped me this time!"

With that, Celes explained the following to me:

The distortion starts off very small, but suddenly expands once it reaches a certain size. I suppose it was like a small hole in a levee bored by ants. Finding distortions before they could rapidly expand was the key to keeping the damage to a minimum.

But, apparently, it was pretty hard to find them while they were still small. Celes had divided up her discarnate entities and used them to search all over, and had given out those crystals for reporting to her to various people, as well.

...It may not have been much, but it was better than nothing.

Once the distortion grew bigger, it could spread from ten to several hundred kilometers at once, ripping open the walls separating our world from adjacent dimensions, causing them to adhere to one another. If the atmospheric pressure between the two worlds was different, the air might come rushing in as violent storms, and most of the organisms in both worlds would die from the sudden extreme changes in weather. There was a chance the air that came over could have been toxic for creatures in the other world, too.

And not only did the worlds adhere to each other, but dimensional tremors and wide-scale destruction involving other neighboring dimensions could occur, as well. It was Celes's job to prevent such disasters. Stopping the course of destruction at one dimension would be a passing mark, while dragging the surrounding worlds into it would be a failure on her part.

She still gets a passing mark even if this world gets destroyed?! That's a scary friggin' thought!

"I've been trying to find them while they're still small, so I can prevent the damage from spreading. If I happen to miss one and it gets big enough to take out all living creatures in a several hundred kilometer radius, that's considered a great success."

"Huh? So even with the incident at Rueda…?"

"Yes, the damage was contained to a very narrow region in that case, so I was able to restore the area afterward. Even though the distortion had grown bigger, that was one of my better handled cases, if I do say so myself. Of course, it's better to deal with the distortion before it can expand, like we did this time. There hasn't been any damage this time, either…"

Celes seemed very happy. Well, there weren't any differences in atmospheric pressure, and it wasn't like there were toxins in the air… now, wait just a minute!

"Celes, there *has* been damage already! And there's way more to come!"

"Whaaat!"

Yes, it was that disease. If anyone thought that was an illness that just happened to occur here by chance instead of something from another world, I'd question their sanity.

"This is the source of the disease that's been going around. I stopped it from spreading at the royal capital and the village near here, but I'm sure it's gotten to other places, too. Since this distortion is the cause of it, this falls under your jurisdiction, right?"

"What? Um… If the disease is caused by the distortion, I suppose…"

Huh, she didn't seem too on board with it.

"That's right! Because of the distortion, pathogens and small infected animals leaked into this world. This is your responsibility to fix! There wasn't much physical damage this time around, so you should focus on restoring things."

"Hmm, that sounds like a lot of work..."

She left me no choice. I was going to use the ace up my sleeve!

"I wonder what the god of Earth would have done. When I talk about what happened here, I'll explain how you..."

"Of course I'll protect the humans from getting harmed by the distortion! That's my duty!"

...Too easy.

"I suppose you... can't send the hosts of the disease back to their original world. Since you already got rid of the distortion. Then I'll need you to completely get rid of all the pests and pathogens that came into this world. Those creatures may only be guilty of being hosts for dangerous pathogens, but it's not impossible that they're also irregular organisms that could totally throw this world's ecosystem out of whack. They could have spread out far and wide, so be sure you don't miss any."

"O-Okay..."

Why was she being so reluctant about this when she was capable of granting me such ridiculous powers? It had to be a simple task for someone as powerful as Celes...

"Elaborate work like this is very troublesome! Do you realize how much effort is needed to get rid of such small animals or pathogens throughout an entire country?! It'd be so much easier to just blow this planet to smithereens, instead!"

Ah, she must have figured out what I was thinking from the look on my face. I doubted she actually read my mind or anything like that.

"Well, good luck. Besides, you just might get praised by the god of Earth if you put in all that effort. He might even say 'good work,' and pat you on the head..."

"There's no time to lose! Okay, I'm going to go work hard to clean this place up! See you later, Kaoru. Thank you so much for today. I'm so glad I have a great friend like you!"

With that, Celes vanished.

"..."

The lieutenant colonel stood there, dumbfounded. It seemed he had returned some time during all of this. The hunter who had guided us there... oh, he was cautiously watching us from a distance.

The others? They were either present the last time Celes had appeared, or they were already used to thinking of me as a goddess, so they didn't seem all that surprised.

...Damn.

"Th-Th-That was..."

"Yup, Celes. Oh, right, she's known as the Goddess Celestine here."

"..."

The lieutenant colonel seemed to be out of service...

"Well, we'll be going now. Thank you for everything, Lieutenant Colonel."

"Wait! Hold on just a minute!!!"

As I tried to leave and say goodbye, the lieutenant colonel raised his voice in a fluster.

"I need you to return to the royal capital! And what about your shop?!"

I wasn't surprised that he didn't want me to go, considering I was on casual speaking terms with the Goddess herself. And I probably seemed far from just an ordinary girl. But I already had an idea of what it would be like if I returned to the royal capital.

So…

"I already canceled the contract for my shop. I cleared out my wares, too, so I have no reason to return to the royal capital. Though, I do have plenty of reasons *not* to go back…"

The lieutenant colonel averted his eyes. Yeah, he already knew exactly what would happen if I went back.

First, I'd get an invitation from the royal palace, then the Temple of the Goddess, influential aristocrats, big-time merchants, and if I went, there'd probably be a bunch of handsome men of marriageable age waiting for me.

…That didn't sound too bad! I mean, never mind!

"No thanks to being a caged bird, swarmed by ants, or being bred! I mean, I do want kids, but only with someone who likes me as a normal girl, and not for my abilities!"

"…Can I ask you one thing?" The lieutenant colonel said with a serious expression. "Where is this 'normal girl' you're talking about?"

"…"

And why exactly are you desperately trying to hold in laughter, Fran, Roland, Emile, and Belle?! You four…

"In any case, you have no right or authority to restrict me from doing what I like. I'm just a traveler who's not from this country, and I'm not a criminal or some foreign spy. Besides, those two over there are nobles from another country. If you tried capturing us by force…"

"Forget nobles from another country, what kind of idiot would try something on someone who has connections with the Goddess Celestine?!"

Well, he had a point.

"But if that's the case, what about the soldier's disease medicine? There are those who haven't been fully cured yet."

"Huh? But even if they did get cured, it'd just come back again, right?"

"…"

I was sure the lieutenant colonel already knew this. He was desperately trying to guilt trip me any way he could, so I would return to the royal capital.

Although I did feel bad about the royal sentries, who seemed happy to finally be free from the soldier's disease.

A lot of their work was pretty repetitive, and they couldn't even scratch themselves, so I would have liked to have helped them.

Like if I made sure they don't catch it agai— Wait a minute!

"Lieutenant Colonel…"

"Hm? What is it?"

"I don't think you'll need to worry about soldier's disease anymore…"

"Huh?"

Yes, I just realized something. What were my thoughts when I created those mini goddess statues?

[Potion that cures and creates antibodies for any epidemic disease going around in the royal capital right now with just a low dose and loses its effectiveness if it's not drunk in twenty-four hours after being scooped, go inside a small container shaped like a goddess statue with an endless generation/circulation system and come out!]

"*…any epidemic disease going around in the royal capital right now…*"

"*…any epidemic disease going around in the royal capital right now…*"

Wouldn't soldier's disease fulfill those conditions? And wouldn't that also mean anyone in the royal capital who drank that medicine would never be afflicted with soldier's disease again? I explained as such to the lieutenant colonel, and...

"What...?"

He was probably disappointed about losing his advantage over other battalions, but he had to be happy that the soldiers would never have to deal with that hated condition ever again.

His face told me he was feeling a mixture of emotions.

"Oh, it's not for certain yet, so please confirm once you get back. And if it's just as I suspect, you can feel free to take all the credit. Just tell them the angel told you to choose your reward, and you wished, not for yourself, but for the sake of everyone else, that the soldier's disease would be eradicated. I'm sure that will increase your prestige among the other soldiers."

There was a forced smile on his face.

"Well, I'll be going now. Oh, and it'll be no use sending anyone after me. No one could catch up to my horses when they've taken my healing potion, and even if they could, they wouldn't be able to keep me from leaving. If anyone tried to use force, Celes would just give 'em a little of that so-called divine punishment..."

"Don't worry, I'll personally report to His Majesty to make sure that won't happen. Our people are well aware of the story of the Goddess Celestine destroying an entire country."

All right, it seemed like I could depart peacefully this time.

"Well then, farewell!"

"..."

Huh? Why was the lieutenant colonel looking at me quizzically?

"What is it?"

"Where do you plan on going now? There's only one guide, and I need him to take me back to the village. Besides, your horses are back at the village. Do you plan on leaving them here and going through the mountains and out onto the road without a guide?"

"Ah…"

The lieutenant colonel looked at me, exasperatedly. Roland and the others, too…

Come on, everyone makes mistakes once in a while!

*　　*

After we retrieved Ed at the village, we started heading east in the opposite direction of the royal capital just as the sun was going down. The plan was to change course to the northeast after moving forward for some time, then head inland.

There was no reason for me to tell the lieutenant colonel this, but it wouldn't be too hard for him to figure out. To the north was Drisard, which we had left behind, to the east was the royal capital, and further beyond that was the kingdom of Brancott, where the prince I disliked was. I was sure he already knew that we had come from that direction. Finally, to the east was the ocean, making it a dead end.

The lieutenant colonel told me that the people from the royal capital should be arriving at the village tomorrow, which was where he'd meet up with them. It was too dangerous for him to wander around the roads at night without having a chemical light like me, so that much was a given. We didn't want to see the people from the royal capital, so we went ahead and marched on through the night.

As soon as the village was no longer visible, I took the carriage out of my Item Box and hopped on.

Now, Fran and Roland, it's time to go.

"U-Um, Kaoru…"

"Hm? What is it?"

As we were about to depart, Francette spoke to me worriedly.

"Um, about that small goddess statue at the royal capital, is it okay for it to keep dispensing medicine like that…?"

Ah, that.

"Don't worry, it has a mechanism built into it so it'll blow up… I mean, shut itself down."

"Shut itself down…?"

"Yup, I made it so it'll break if someone tries to steal it or if it fulfills its purpose, so no need to worry! Okay, let's go!"

And so, we headed east.

We were going to continue in that direction until we reached the road leading northward, and then head inland.

…Oh, but maybe we wouldn't be able to eat seafood if we took the inland route? Maybe we should go all the way around to the coast, instead? There wasn't a particular destination for our journey, so it didn't really matter where we went, anyway.

All right, change of plans. First we'll head south toward the ocean, then head east! Time to eat sashimi for the first time in a while! How wonderful it was to not have to worry about pathogens, toxins, or parasites!

It was also wonderful that I could create healing potions that tasted like soy sauce and disinfectants that tasted like wasabi! Yes, it's time for a journey in search of coastal cities!

"Hiyo, Silver!"

"Again, what horse are you talking about?!"

*　　*

"Stand aside! That belongs at the royal palace!"

"Nonsense! The miracle statue of the Goddess should be protected by the Temple of the Goddess! You are the ones who must stand down!"

"Now, wait just a minute! We have been tasked to protect these two statues by the Angel herself. Their blessings must be bestowed to the people freely and equally. The royal palace and temple have no right to take them to be used for their own political and monetary gain!"

Three groups of men stood arguing at the central plaza of the royal capital in front of the Goddess statue. They were civil servants from the royal capital and the royal sentries that escorted them, priests from the Temple of the Goddess, and the men who Kaoru had tasked with managing the mini goddess statues until they had fulfilled their purpose. None of them seemed to have any intention of giving an inch.

This was no surprise. The royal palace and the temple would have surrendered their authority if they backed down here. In fact, they'd be lucky if that was the only thing they lost. Meanwhile, the men who Kaoru had entrusted with managing things there couldn't even fathom abandoning the duty assigned to them.

The royal capital's citizens watched the rather austere scene for a while longer, until the men from the royal palace lost their patience and put their hands on one of the mini goddess statues. It seemed they were planning on taking it by force. Seeing this, the priests hurriedly took hold of the other statue.

The men who had been appointed couldn't put their hands on the priests or men of the royal palace, so all they could do was yell out profanities. And just as the sentries from the royal palace gently lifted the medicine-dispensing mini goddess statue…

Crack!

It shattered into pieces.

"Huh...?"

The men of the royal palace stared blankly at the fragments on the ground that used to be the mini goddess statue.

"Now do you see?! The Goddess would not allow a statue in her image to fall into the hands of impure ones. This miracle will be managed by us, the Temple of the Goddess, and—"

The highest-ranking priest spoke as he lifted the other statue, which also shattered into pieces. It clearly wasn't because he held it wrong or anything like that. It broke in a way that seemed physically impossible. The statues had been completely reduced to smithereens. The pieces had been broken so finely that it was impossible to discern what their original form could have been. It was a clear sign that the Goddess was not pleased.

"..."

Silence fell over the central plaza. Then the countless eyes of the wordless crowd stared daggers into the men from the palace and temple with looks of anger, hatred, and contempt.

Through her Angel, the Goddess had blessed the people with a statue of miracles. And this statue had saved the inhabitants of the royal capital with the never-ending medicine pot it was holding. Because the vile men of the royal palace and rotten priests had ignored her wishes and tried to take them for themselves, those miracles were now gone. Forever.

The men of the royal palace and priests stood frozen, sweating profusely as many eyes stared directly at them.

"The Lady Angel had asked us to handle things here until the mini goddess statues had fulfilled their duties. Now, due to men with tainted hearts attempting to take them away, the goddess statue no longer exists. In other words, they have fulfilled their duties. And so… our duty, too, has ended. It's only been two days and nights, but it was an honor to fulfill the Angel's orders. You can all take responsibility for the rest. Now, to those who have helped me in this task, let us pass down stories of our accomplishments here with pride to our descendants. Disband!"

It seemed the individual who'd taken charge of the group was someone of status. Perhaps he was a noble who happened to be hanging out in the city in commoner clothes, but after giving his uncommoner-like speech, he quickly vanished into the rest of the crowd. The rest quickly followed.

Before the men of the royal palace and priests knew it, they were the only ones surrounded by the crowd.

…We have to run.

The thought crossed their minds, but they couldn't just go back empty handed.

Without any options left, they gathered the pieces of the mini goddess statue as holy relics to take back, but it was unlikely that they would ever be publicly displayed as such. Because in order to explain why they were in such a state, they had to explain their own foolish behavior and admit their actions had been rejected by the Goddess.

If they're planning on putting all the blame on us subordinates, we're taking down the higher-ups who ordered us to take the statue by force for their own personal gain with us.

Such were the thoughts of the men who were retrieving the statue fragments while on the verge of tears. Everyone, on both the royal palace and temple sides…

Meanwhile, at the royal palace and temple, news from the east village had been delivered by the soldier who departed the previous day, and preparations for a grand celebration were being made in a great hurry.

The appearance of the Angel and a miraculous revelation. Not to mention the Angel was there, at the royal capital of the kingdom of Jusral. It went without saying that the royalty, titled nobility, and religious parties were ecstatic to receive the news.

The Angel had saved the royal capital from the horrid disease and headed to the village that was thought to be where it originated to save the people there. Once she completed her task, she would return to the royal capital. Envoys had already been sent to greet her, and they would surely depart from the village to head toward the royal capital by the next morning.

When the Angel arrived at the royal capital, they would greet her with a splendid welcome, show their gratitude, and… gain her favor. Each of those with high standing in the political and religious fields were picturing a bright future ahead. The only people of this nation that knew the girl wasn't going to return to the royal capital was the third son of a noble house who she called the Lieutenant Colonel, and the realtor who she had canceled the lease agreement with.

The lieutenant colonel still hadn't returned to the royal capital, and the realtor was late in arriving at the central plaza, so he still didn't realize the girl who canceled the lease to leave the royal capital and the Angel were one in the same.

*　　*

"I wonder if the mini goddess statue is still okay..."

That statue-type potion creation device was created so it would automatically break apart after five days. There was no way she would have left a device that would continue dispensing potions forever. Even if the effects were limited to epidemic diseases, I didn't want some idiot to start claiming that their country was protected by the blessing of the Goddess! It would be like that ruined religious state all over again.

Besides, medical effects aside, even an item that creates an infinite supply of drinking water could have been valuable in itself to the army. It might've spawned some religious fanatics who thought their army was protected by the Goddess and her blessed water. That's why I made them so they would disintegrate without a trace, to prevent them from being taken advantage of later.

And even if five days hadn't passed yet, I made it so they would self-destruct the moment someone tried to move them. If someone moved one and it broke in such an unnatural fashion, I doubted they would try to touch the other one afterward. I doubted they would ever be left completely alone with them being in such a visible location, so a random thief wouldn't be able to get their hands on them either.

The only people who could touch them openly in front of watching eyes would be those from the royal palace or Temple of the Goddess. So, at least one of them should survive until the full five-day time limit was up.

But that was before I thought about getting Celes to help, and now that she was going to get rid of the source of the disease, the statues were no longer needed. It wouldn't be an issue if they both broke now. If the statues break not because of the time limit, but because someone tried to take them, they'd be in pretty big trouble, but that didn't concern me. It'd be their own fault in that case.

"Kaoru, we'll be reaching the road that branches off to the north and south. You want to keep moving toward the east, right?" Francette turned toward me and asked.

She was able to see what was coming up before me, since she had a higher vantage point on horseback while I was behind the canopy.

...Come to think of it, Francette's eyesight was enhanced with my potions. She was probably seeing things at a distance that wouldn't normally be possible for humans. Disregarding obstacles and the terrain, and the fact that the world was round.

"Oh, we won't be going east until we hit the ocean, so we'll be going south there first. It'd be more fun to travel along the coast than going inland!"

Without any specific destination in mind, no one had any reason to protest. For now, we'd be heading south. We'd travel the coast and enjoy some seafood as we journeyed along the outskirts of the continent. All in search of a place to live safely and a companion for reproduction.

Regardless of Francette and Roland, I absolutely couldn't let Emile and Belle beat me to it in that regard. This journey is about expanding the Nagase bloodline, not yours!

And Roland and Francette's horses! You'd better not be trying to get with Ed's daughter!

What am I gonna do with them...

ACK!

Extra: Meanwhile, at the Royal Capital...

Boxed Meal Shop Regulars

"I want that boxed lunch..."

"I want some simmered mushrooms..."

"I want a meal cooked by girls..."

The customers who used to be regulars at Layette's Atelier for their boxed lunches were now at the bread shop that replaced it, grumbling to themselves as they browsed the options.

When Layette's Atelier closed down, a quick-witted bread shop employee immediately rented out the spot and went independent. They began offering boxed lunches and side dishes along with bread to inherit the customers of Layette's Atelier. However...

"Well, it's not bad, but..."

"Compared to Layette's Atelier..."

The shop owner may have been an employee at a bread shop before, but he wasn't eating bread three meals a day every day.

So when he was working at his former workplace, he had eaten the meals from Layette's Atelier several times.

That was how he came up with the idea of offering boxed lunches and side dishes along with bread as soon as he had heard about it closing, and he quickly made a move to rent out the location and retain the old customers.

The old regulars who had no time to prepare lunch were accustomed to the convenient nutritious boxed meals, but they couldn't help but compare the new offerings to those at Layette's Atelier.

Not to mention, Kaoru had stocked her ingredients at the market, but the seasonings and condiments were created with her ability.

Soy sauce, miso, black pepper, cayenne pepper, salt, sugar, etc.

Many of them were either ridiculously expensive or unavailable altogether in this country.

...There was no way to compete.

The regulars were also used to the filling meals that came with rice, and the bread-based meals offered now left them feeling unsatisfied.

But with the owner being a baker, he couldn't help but put the focus on bread for economic and other reasons.

"Aw man... Why'd Kaoru and the girls have to go..."

"She had no choice. She was the Angel, after all... If she did come back after all that, there was no way she could keep running her shop. The royalty, nobles, and rotten priests from the temple would never leave her alone..."

"I wish she would've kept selling boxed lunches as the ordinary girl with scary eyes instead of the Angel..."

"Idiot, then the royal capital and the rest of the country would still be infested with the epidemic!"

"I'm sorry I couldn't meet your expectations..."

The owner lowered his head apologetically as he rang up a customer at the counter.

Since he was a former customer of Kaoru's meals himself, he knew full well that his were no match.

He was in his mid-twenties and leapt at the chance to build the new business that was a fusion of a bread, boxed lunch and side dishes shop, and didn't have sufficient funds to hire any workers.

All his savings had been used up on renovations, a baker's oven, and other expenses.

His funds were actually a bit insufficient, and he had some outstanding loans.

He couldn't stop sending money to his family that needed his support either.

"Well, it's much better than not having a shop like this at all. Don't beat yourself up over it..."

One of the customers realized he may have been too harsh and tried to cheer up the owner.

"But it's a guy making these..."

"If it was a little girl, or at least a young woman..."

Other customers continued to complain, but with no funds to hire employees, there was nothing that could be done.

Unless the owner could get married and have a daughter or something.

The owner stood there looking glum, when the doorbell rang with a cling...

Three girls, aged sixteen to seventeen, twelve to thirteen, and seven to eight, leapt into the shop together.

"Hey Big Brother, we heard you got your own shop!"

"You have open rooms, right? We wanted to live in the royal capit— I mean..."

"We're here to help!"

"Girls!!!"

The customers seemed ecstatic, but the owner looked pale.

The oldest and second oldest of his younger sisters were terrible at cooking.

But they were unaware of this fact, and would often try to cook for their family.

The reason the shop owner went to the royal capital wasn't just to become successful there, but a lot of it had to do with escaping the cooking his sisters made at home.

The youngest of the three wasn't old enough to entrust with cooking either.

All he could do was pray her cooking skills wouldn't take after her sisters'.

The young owner watched the rejoicing customers, deep in thought.

"If my sisters have anything to do with the food I put out, my shop is done for..."

There would be many hardships ahead of him.

Soldiers of the Royal Capital

"What, the soldier's disease is never coming back again?"

"It's thanks to the second battalion commander!"

"Three cheers for Lieutenant Colonel Vonsas!"

"Hip hip, hooray!!!"

The lieutenant colonel was exploding in popularity.

"But who would've thought that girl from the medicine shop was the Angel..."

"I knew she couldn't be an ordinary girl when I saw those powerful eyes..."

Actually, she just had naturally scary-looking eyes.

Then…

"Those in the royal army were immune to soldier's disease."

As such rumors spread, people from the country began going out of their way to join the royal army instead of the military of their liege lord, and immediately contracted soldier's disease upon joining.

Even though their seniors and colleagues who were originally from the royal capital were completely free of the affliction.

"This isn't what I signed up for!"

There was no point in complaining.

As a result, there was an awkward and sensitive rift in the royal army between the natives of the royal capital and those from the country. But at this point, no one knew that this would contribute to stronger solidarity for those from the country.

Over ten years later, the royal army of the kingdom of Jusral would face a grave problem.

As more people who hadn't drank from the mini goddess statue back then joined the royal army, soldier's disease began spreading quickly among the ranks of even new soldiers who were born in the royal capital.

Even though their seniors who were also born in the royal capital were immune, soldier's disease was spreading among their ranks at an explosive rate.

Over the span of ten years, it had become known that soldier's disease only occurred among those who weren't born in the royal capital, but this common knowledge had been thoroughly debunked.

This led to the sentiment that the citizens of the royal capital were no longer blessed by the goddess, and the higher-ups of the army and royal palace were at a loss for what to do…

The Royal Capital and Temple of the Goddess

"Whaaat?!"

The king, who was usually so mild-mannered, raised his voice angrily as he rose from his seat.

This was already an abnormal situation in and of itself.

"They tried to take the goddess statue for themselves and ended up destroying both statues? And the royal palace and temple sides broke one each? Preposterous! There may still be sick people in neighboring cities! What's going to happen to them now?! And whose orders were they acting on in the first place?!"

The news was too much for the king to bear without losing his composure.

"D-Does this mean our Goddess Celestine has forsaken us? Has she given up on us as blasphemous fools...? At least we haven't angered her so much that she destroys the kingdom... no, that's not the issue here! Wh-What do we do...?"

The king was anxious at first, but the disease didn't spread in the cities or villages afterward, and the goddess didn't bring judgment down upon them.

The royal palace had lost some of its dignity, but it wasn't as if there were elections for them to worry about.

This event ended up not being big enough to spark anything like a rebellion in a kingdom that didn't have competition for the right of succession, and so the king was relieved.

Meanwhile, at the Temple of the Goddess...

The archbishop received the news from his bishop, and his usually holy and gentle face was contorted fiercely as he screamed.

"Wh-Wh-Whaaaaaat?!"

They had ignored the orders of the Angel and greedily tried to take the miraculous statue from the goddess.

The goddess had rejected them, and the statues were destroyed as a result.

Even though there could still be sick people in cities and villages outside of the royal capital.

It wasn't as bad for the royal palace.

They would just look bad and get some criticism from the people.

The whole thing would be forgotten in no time.

But it wasn't so simple for the temple.

Priests had ignored the words of the Angel, tried to take the statue by force, and got rejected by the goddess.

While it wouldn't damage the peoples' fear and faith for the goddess, it would be a definite blow to the respect, trust, and donations for the Temple of the Goddess.

And a significant one at that…

"Wh-Who was it! Who's responsible for giving such an order?!"

"I-It was Father Haramous!"

Father Haramous.

He was a troublesome and worldly-minded priest who cared far too much about money and power.

He likely gave the order to his acolytes in an attempt to gain some merit for himself.

"Father Haramous… You've done it now…"

In that moment, Haramous's chances of advancing his career had been completely killed off.

The archbishop looked at the "holy artifact" that was handed to him, which was a mere collection of fragments and powder, and slumped his shoulders.

"I suppose what's done is done. Now we'll have to bring the Angel to the temple so we can apologize and make up for this by having her bestow a miracle or blessing upon us. Then we can tell the people that the goddess has granted us forgiveness. Now, prepare for a welcoming ceremony! Don't hesitate to spend money!"

And so, the royal palace and temple made preparations for a lavish welcoming ceremony, and the convoys from both sides glared at each other at the entrance of the royal capital.

They were competing over who would invite the Angel to their side first.

It was a heavy responsibility, and the cost for failure was similarly heavy.

"Urrrgh..."

The two factions continued glaring at each other.

However, there was still no sign of the Angel and the men sent to receive her.

The citizens of the royal capital looked at them with disdain as they walked by.

The long, long wait for the men was just beginning.

The crowd of men continued standing at the royal palace and temple with eyes full of expectation and hope...

The Orphanage

When Kaoru was delivering gifts to the orphanage and street urchins, a thought once crossed her mind.

Wasn't she only providing temporary relief and satisfying her own ego?

Orphans weren't exclusive to the royal capital.

And of course, they weren't exclusive to just this country.

She wasn't going to be around forever, either.

It was possible that she'd find someone at the capital to settle down with, but there were no such plans at that point.

What would happen if she was to leave suddenly?

Or what if she slips through Celes's protection, which was dubious in the first place, and died or became unable to take action?

The kids at the orphanage would still be able to survive on their own, and achieve relative happiness by their own accord.

Though that did depend on the individual, and not all of them would make it.

With street urchins, it was uncertain whether they'd be able to make it to the starting line of adulthood.

But granting some ridiculous blessing to children just because they're orphans wouldn't help them in the long run.

They would become a target for the envious, or they could make them arrogant and lose their good nature.

So Kaoru decided to raise their odds of survival by juuust a bit and leave it at that.

"Immunity to food poisoning even when eating rotten or toxic foods."

"The ability to absorb nutrients by eating weeds."

"The ability to absorb pathogens and parasites and turn them into nutrients."

...Pretty weak.

They weren't much of a blessing to a normal commoner, and it was unlikely for anyone to find out about such minor things.

...In fact, they probably wouldn't notice it themselves.

But for a street urchin, it was a "blessing from God" that would greatly decrease the hurdles of surviving into adulthood, which was fifteen years old.

Even if that person was never aware of their own blessing.

Kaoru had secretly included potions with such effects in the food she'd been delivering as gifts.

(This should help increase their odds a little even if I'm not around...)

Then, the incident regarding the "distortions" occurred.

It pained Kaoru to leave without saying goodbye to the children who had grown so close to her, but life was a cycle of meetings and partings.

Though they may have only crossed paths for a fleeting moment, it would be enough for Kaoru if she was able to help their chances of survival even a little.

With those thoughts in mind, she put the royal capital behind her.

Meanwhile, at the royal palace…

"What? The Angel is missing?! She never returned from the village in the east? Her shop in the royal palace is already emptied out? Find her! Find the Angel nooow!!!"

Meanwhile, at the Temple of the Goddess…

"Find her! Bring the Angel back, no matter what it takes! Oh, but be gentle with her! Do not do anything that could incur the wrath of the Goddess Celestine!"

But the search for the Angel ended in failure.

Then they thought about it.

After doing all sorts of research, they heard the Angel had taken care of children at the orphanage by giving them work and sending them gifts.

If that's the case, perhaps she would be impressed by efforts to save the orphans.

Then, if they do find the Angel or she returns some day, they could invite her to discuss the charity work for the orphanage.

There was no way she wouldn't accept that invite, and she'd be open to hearing them out!

It was the perfect plan!

And so, the country and temple began supporting the orphanage. The maximum capacity was increased as they expanded the facilities, and the street urchins were taken in as well.

The orphans weren't stupid. They heard what the adults were talking about, and understood who was responsible for the improvement of their conditions. Though, even if that hadn't happened, it wouldn't have changed where their loyalties lay.

And eventually, everyone stopped using whistles in the royal capital. Anyone who blew a whistle would attract orphans from all over the royal capital. They would rush over, excitedly shouting that Lady Kaoru had returned...

It was a scary sight to see dozens of orphans running toward you, but it was heartbreaking to see them walk away disappointed with slumped shoulders.

Eventually, the orphans became known as the Servants of the Goddess...

Hello, this is FUNA.

I'd like to sincerely thank you for picking up this title!

This brings the second season of I Shall Survive Using Potions! to a close.

Since I was bringing back a title that had wrapped up once already, I was prepared to receive comments saying, "It would have been better to end it at the first one," and I actually did receive those comments, but I also had a lot of people who wanted to read more, so I decided to go through with it.

You know, it's kind of like the sentiment of, "I won't destroy the town of Sodom if there are fifty people there with righteous hearts."

So, if there are fifty people who would want to read the continuation of the series, I wanted to write it for them.

Reader: There might only be ten of us.
FUNA: I'll write it for those ten people.
Editor: We wouldn't publish it in that case, though.
FUNA: Gyaaaaaa!!!

Since the next volume is out, I hope it sells well!

Volume three will be coming out this month, as well as volume two of the manga!

To my editor; the illustrator, Sukima; the binding designer; the proofreader; and others, the printer, distributor, and bookstores; the light novel submission website, Shōsetsuka ni Narō; everyone who pointed out errors or provided advice in the feedback section; and everyone who picked up this book, I appreciate you all from the bottom of my heart.

Thank you!

I would be thrilled if you continue to support the light novel and manga.

I hope to see you again in the next volume…

4
Author
FUNA
SUKI
I SHALL SURVIVE USING POTIONS!
NOVEL VOLUME 4
ON SALE
MARCH 2021!

riginal Work: FUNA
anga: Hibiki Kokonoe
aracter Design: Sukima
I SHALL SURVIVE USING POTIONS!
2
MANGA VOLUME 2
ON SALE
JANUARY 2021!

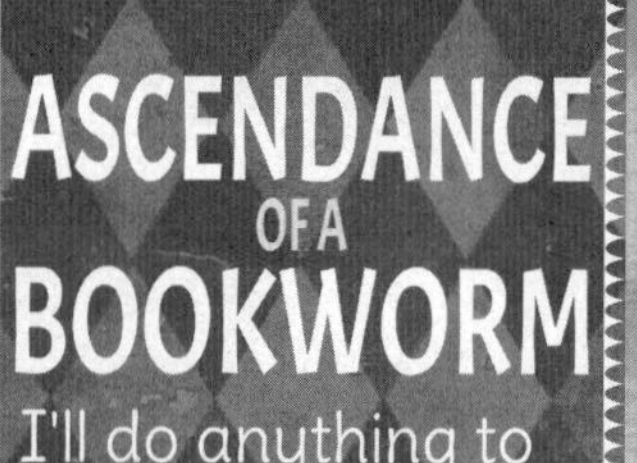
ASCENDANCE
OF A
BOOKWORM
I'll do anything to become a librarian!
Part 2 Apprentice Shrine Maiden Vol. 4
Author: Miya Kazuki
Illustrator: You Shiina

Artist: Kami Imai
Original Author: Sakon Kaidou
Character Designs: Taiki
MANGA OMNIBUS 1
ON SALE NOW!
1
Infinite Dendrogram

Gamei Hitsuji
illustration=Yuunagi
The Magic in this Other World is Too Far Behind!
9
Volume 9
On Sale Now!!

novel
club

J-Novel Club Lineup

Ebook Releases Series List

A Lily Blooms in Another World
A Wild Last Boss Appeared!
Altina the Sword Princess
Amagi Brilliant Park
An Archdemon's Dilemma: How to Love Your Elf Bride
Arifureta Zero
Arifureta: From Commonplace to World's Strongest
Ascendance of a Bookworm
Beatless
Bibliophile Princess
Black Summoner
By the Grace of the Gods
Campfire Cooking in Another World with My Absurd Skill
Can Someone Please Explain What's Going On?!
Cooking with Wild Game
Crest of the Stars
Deathbound Duke's Daughter
Demon Lord, Retry!
Der Werwolf: The Annals of Veight
From Truant to Anime Screenwriter: My Path to "Anohana" and "The Anthem of the Heart"
Full Metal Panic!
Grimgar of Fantasy and Ash
Her Majesty's Swarm
Holmes of Kyoto
How a Realist Hero Rebuilt the Kingdom
How NOT to Summon a Demon Lord
I Refuse to Be Your Enemy!
I Saved Too Many Girls and Caused the Apocalypse
I Shall Survive Using Potions!
In Another World With My Smartphone
Infinite Dendrogram
Infinite Stratos
Invaders of the Rokujouma!?
Isekai Rebuilding Project
JK Haru is a Sex Worker in Another World
Kobold King
Kokoro Connect
Last and First Idol
Lazy Dungeon Master
Mapping: The Trash-Tier Skill That Got Me Into a Top-Tier Party
Middle-Aged Businessman, Arise in Another World!
Mixed Bathing in Another Dimension
Monster Tamer
My Big Sister Lives in a Fantasy World
My Instant Death Ability is So Overpowered, No One in This Other World Stands a Chance Against Me!
My Next Life as a Villainess: All Routes Lead to Doom!
Otherside Picnic
Outbreak Company
Outer Ragna
Record of Wortenia War
Seirei Gensouki: Spirit Chronicles
Sexiled: My Sexist Party Leader Kicked Me Out, So I Teamed Up With a Mythical Sorceress!
Slayers
Sorcerous Stabber Orphen: The Wayward Journey
Tearmoon Empire
Teogonia
The Bloodline
The Combat Butler and Automaton Waitress
The Economics of Prophecy
The Epic Tale of the Reincarnated Prince Herscherik
The Extraordinary, the Ordinary, and SOAP!
The Greatest Magicmaster's Retirement Plan
The Holy Knight's Dark Road
The Magic in this Other World is Too Far Behind!
The Master of Ragnarok & Blesser of Einherjar
The Sorcerer's Receptionist
The Tales of Marielle Clarac
The Underdog of the Eight Greater Tribes
The Unwanted Undead Adventurer
WATARU!! The Hot-Blooded Fighting Teen & His Epic Adventures in a Fantasy World After Stopping a Truck with His Bare Hands!!
The White Cat's Revenge as Plotted from the Demon King's Lap
The World's Least Interesting Master Swordsman
Welcome to Japan, Ms. Elf!
When the Clock Strikes Z
Wild Times with a Fake Fake Princess

Manga Series:

A Very Fairy Apartment
An Archdemon's Dilemma: How to Love Your Elf Bride
Animeta!
Ascendance of a Bookworm
Bibliophile Princess
Black Summoner
Campfire Cooking in Another World with My Absurd Skill
Cooking with Wild Game
Demon Lord, Retry!
Discommunication
How a Realist Hero Rebuilt the Kingdom
I Love Yuri and I Got Bodyswapped with a Fujoshi!
I Shall Survive Using Potions!
Infinite Dendrogram
Mapping: The Trash-Tier Skill That Got Me Into a Top-Tier Party
Marginal Operation
Record of Wortenia War
Seirei Gensouki: Spirit Chronicles
Sorcerous Stabber Orphen: The Reckless Journey
Sorcerous Stabber Orphen: The Youthful Journey
Sweet Reincarnation
The Faraway Paladin
The Magic in this Other World is Too Far Behind!
The Master of Ragnarok & Blesser of Einherjar
The Tales of Marielle Clarac
The Unwanted Undead Adventurer

Keep an eye out at j-novel.club for further new title announcements!